Contents

Easy Custard Cake Filling ....

Easy Cream Cheese Frosting 7

Microwave Scrambled Eggs 8

Brown Sugar and Pineapple Glazed Ham 8

Doughnut in a Mug 9

Microwave Caramel Popcorn 10

Semi-Indulgent Easy Brown Rice 11

Soft-Boiled Eggs in the Microwave 11

Cinnamon Apples 12

Keto Peanut Butter Fudge Fat Bomb 13

Keto Cocoa Mug Cake 13

Mocha Truffles 14

Pumpkin Pie Mug Cake 15

Can't Wait Microwave Lava Cake 16

Whole Wheat Cereal Bars 17

Southwest Squash Casserole 17

Bangan ka Bhurta (Indian Eggplant) 18

Peachy Oatmeal 18

Microwaved Potatoes Lyonnaise 19

Ridiculously Easy Queso Fresco "Dip" 20

Individual Microwave Brownie 20

Vegan Mug Cake with Pineapple and Mint 21

Easy Frozen Hot Chocolate 22

Coffee Mug Cake 22

Microwave Pecan Brittle 23

Easy Butter Fingers Candy 24

Spanish Rice (Microwave) 25

Microwave Peanut Butter Chocolate Swirl Fudge 25

BBQ Potatoes with Green Onions 26

S'mores Rice Crispy Treats 27

Jicama Zebra Fries 27

Quick Peach Cobbler In a Mug....28
Easy Turkish Delight....29
Vegan Mug Cake....29
Lazy Green Peas....30
Paleo One-Minute MuffinPeanut Butter Popcorn....31
Minute Chocolate Mug Cake....31
Blueberry, Coconut, and Pistachio Chocolate Bark....32
Microwave Apple Kugel....33
Microwave Baked Apples....34
Mocha Truffles....35
PB and J Mini Mug Cakes....36
Fudgy Nutella Mug Cake....37
Shorecook's Cashew Brittle....37
Individual Microwave Brownie....38
Microwave Apple Crisp....39
No-Egg Blueberry Mug Cake....40
Microwave Scalloped Potatoes....40
189.2 calories; protein 5.4g 11% DV; carbohydrates 31g 10% DV; fat 5.2g 8% DV; cholesterol 15.1mg 5% DV; sodium 836.8mg 34% DV....41
Beets with Mandarin Oranges....42
Taco Lasagna with Noodles....42
Chocolate Marshmallow Fondant....43
Easy Microwave Maple Fudge....44
Chili Cheese Dip V....45
Hasty Chocolate Pudding....45
Potato Chips....46
Microwave Baked Potato....47
Southwest Chicken Casserole....47
Microwave Oven Peanut Brittle....48
Shelby's Microwave Meat Loaf....49
Schweineruckbraten (Microwave Loin of Pork)....49
Basic Microwave Risotto....50
Gourmet Microwave Popcorn....51

Microwave Corn on the Cob 51
Microwave Chocolate Mug Cake 52
White Cranberry Walnut Nutmeg Fudge 52
Microwave Lemon Curd 53
Microwave Peanut Butter Chocolate Swirl Fudge 54
Mom's Goulash in the Microwave 55
World's Best Bacon Cheese Dip 56
Easy Microwave Chilaquiles 57
Broccoli Cheese Soup VIII 57
Jalapeno Popper Spread 58
Sesame Udon Noodles 58
Cheesy Chicken and Rice Casserole 59
Cinnamon Sugar Tortilla Delight 60
Microwave English Muffin Bread 61
Lemon Cake in a Mug 62
Microwave Raisin Bread Pudding 62
Cindy's Microwave Chicken Parmesan 63
Butternut Soup 64
Banana Nut Oatmeal 65
Scrambled Eggs in a Mug 65
Easy Glazed Carrots 66
Freeze-and-Reheat Breakfast Burritos 66
Quick and Easy Grilled Potatoes 67
Instant Chocolate Hard Shell 68
Corn on the Cob in the Microwave 68
Microwave Nutella Mug Cake 69
Corn On The Cob (Easy Cleaning and Shucking) 69
Simple French Toast in a Cup 70
Easy Mochi 71
No Egg Chocolate Mug Cake 71
90-Second Keto Bread in a Mug 72
Fluffy Microwave Scrambled Eggs 73
Microwave Popcorn 73

Microwave Corn-on-the-Cob in the Husk 74
Quick and Simple Broccoli and Cheese 74
Grilled Asian Chicken 75
Easy Microwave Chocolate Cake 76
Microwave Bread and Butter Pickles 77
Microwave Mochi 77
Loaded Potato Soup I 78
PBM Sandwich 79
Homemade Pumpkin Puree in the Microwave 79
BBQ Chicken Chopped Salad 80
Apple Crisp in a Mug 81
Twice Microwaved Potatoes 82
Buttery Lemon Spinach 83
Single-Serve Blueberry Crisp 83
Avocado and Black Bean Dip 84
Easy Microwave Peanut Brittle 84
Easy Brownie In A Mug 85
Super Simple Perfect Chocolate Ganache 86
Microwave Spiced Nuts 86
Brownie In a Mug 87
Mayan Hot Chocolate 88
Chocolate Shell Sauce 88
Cheesy Cauliflower in the Microwave 88
Easy, Fast Chocolate Cup Muffin 89
Candied Acorn Squash 90
Apple Butter the Easy Way Microwave Macaroni and Cheese 90
Chocolate Covered Blueberries 91
Celery Salt 91
Mom's Goulash in the Microwave 92
10-Minute Chocolate Mug Cake 93
Gaye's Microwave Fudge 94
PB and J Mini Mug Cakes 94
S'more Pie 95

Sweet Sticky Rice with Mangoes 97
Creamy Chicken Tortilla Bake 98
The Best Steamed Asparagus 99
Easy Egg White Omelet 99
Microwave Cake 100
Crispy Peanut Butter Chocolate Log 100
Jalapeno Chicken Dip 102
Microwave Pralines 102
Chocolaty Peanut Butter Haystacks 103
Brown Rice, Broccoli, Cheese and Walnut Surprise 103
Twice-Baked Ranch Potatoes 104
Chocolate Ice Cream Mug Cake 105
Mexican Chocolate/Salted Caramel Cake in a Mug 105
Microwave Vegetables 106
Simple Microwave Peanut Brittle 107
Lemon Drop Bark 107
Denny's Amazing Five Minute Asiago Dip 108
Dill-Pickled Cherry Tomatoes 108
Scottish Pudding 109
Stuffed Acorn Squash Supreme 110
Lemon Mug Cake 111
Chicken Enchiladas III 111
Spooky Halloween Eyeballs 112
Escargot Mushrooms 113
Easy Cashew Sea Salt Toffee 114
The Best White Chocolate Almond Bark 115
Asparagus Lasagna 115
Miracle Chocolate-Coffee Icing Green Tea Mousse Cheesecake 116
Easy Spicy Udon Cold Salad 117
Keto Peanut Butter Bars 118
Black Bean Soup with Bacon 119
Movie Theater Floor 120
Dan's Meat Wrap 121

Chocolate Hummus 121
Espresso Bark....... 122
Lavender Truffles....... 123
Corn with Jalapenos 123
Milky Way Cupcake Icing....... 124
139.9 calories; protein 0.7g 1% DV; carbohydrates 21.4g 7% DV; fat 5.8g 9% DV; cholesterol 9.6mg 3% DV; sodium 48.2mg 2% DV....... 124
Keto Potato Salad 125
Unbelievable Vegan Mashed Potatoes....... 126
Texas Hash in the Microwave....... 126
Candy Bar Fudge....... 127
Zucchini Dutch Cheese Casserole 128
Leftover Dog Pile 129
Plantains in Butter Rum Sauce 129
Peanut Butter Cups....... 130
White Chocolate-Raspberry Ganache 131
Bella's Mac and Cheese 131
Chicken Cabbage Wraps 132

Easy Custard Cake Filling

Prep: 5 mins **Cook:** 8 mins **Additional:** 30 mins **Total:** 43 mins **Servings:** 8 **Yield:** 2 cups approximately

Ingredients

- 2 cups milk
- ¾ cup white sugar
- 5 tablespoons all-purpose flour
- ¼ teaspoon salt
- 2 large eggs eggs
- 1 teaspoon vanilla extract

Directions

Step 1

Heat milk in microwave-safe glass or ceramic bowl in the microwave on high until hot but not boiling, 2 to 4 minutes. Combine sugar, flour, and salt together in a separate microwave-safe glass or ceramic bowl. Whisk hot milk into the sugar mixture gradually. Cook milk mixture in microwave on high in 1-minute intervals, stirring after each interval, until thickened, 4 to 5 minutes.

Step 2

Whisk eggs in a separate small bowl until pale and frothy. Whisk 1/3 cup of the milk mixture into eggs gradually, then whisk egg mixture into remaining milk mixture gradually until smooth custard forms. Heat custard in microwave on high until thickened, about 2 minutes more. Cool slightly; stir in vanilla extract. Chill custard in refrigerator until completely cooled, about 30 minutes.

Nutrition Facts

Per Serving:

140.3 calories; protein 4.1g 8% DV; carbohydrates 25.5g 8% DV; fat 2.5g 4% DV; cholesterol 51.4mg 17% DV; sodium 115.3mg 5% DV.

Easy Cream Cheese Frosting

Prep: 15 mins **Total:** 15 mins **Servings:** 15 **Yield:** 2 -1/2 cups

Ingredients

- ½ cup butter
- 6 ounces cream cheese, softened
- 2 teaspoons vanilla extract
- 2 cups confectioners' sugar

Directions

Step 1

Heat butter in a microwave-safe dish in microwave on high for 7 seconds. Transfer butter to a bowl and beat with cream cheese and vanilla extract with an electric mixer until mixture is nearly fluffy, about 5 minutes. Gradually stir confectioners' sugar into cream cheese mixture to make a smooth frosting. Store in refrigerator.

Nutrition Facts

Per Serving:

160.5 calories; protein 0.9g 2% DV; carbohydrates 17g 6% DV; fat 10.1g 16% DV; cholesterol 28.7mg 10% DV; sodium 77.4mg 3% DV.

Microwave Scrambled Eggs

Prep: 2 mins **Cook:** 3 mins **Total:** 5 mins **Servings:** 4 **Yield:** 4 servings

Ingredients

- 1 cooking spray
- 8 eaches eggs
- 1 pinch salt and ground black pepper to taste

Directions

Step 1

Spray a large glass bowl with cooking spray. Crack 1 egg into a small ramekin and then pour into the bowl. Whisk egg. Repeat with remaining eggs, whisking well after each addition.

Step 2

Cook eggs in a microwave oven for 30 seconds; remove from oven and stir. Continue cooking in 30-second intervals, stirring after each, until eggs are almost set, about 3 minutes total. Season with salt and pepper.

Nutrition Facts

Per Serving:

126.4 calories; protein 11.1g 22% DV; carbohydrates 0.7g; fat 8.8g 14% DV; cholesterol 327.4mg 109% DV; sodium 162mg 7% DV.

Brown Sugar and Pineapple Glazed Ham

Prep: 20 mins **Cook:** 1 hr 30 mins **Total:** 1 hr 50 mins **Servings:** 20 **Yield:** 1 6-pound glazed ham

Ingredients

- 1 (6 pound) fully-cooked, bone-in ham
- 1 fresh pineapple
- 2 (6 ounce) cans pineapple juice
- 1 cup brown sugar

Directions

Step 1

Preheat oven to 325 degrees F (165 degrees C). Place the ham, cut side down, into a roasting pan.

Step 2

Cut the skin off the pineapple with a sharp knife and cut out any brown spots of skin left behind. Slice the pineapple into 1/2-inch slices and cut the cores out of the slices. Pin the slices onto the ham with toothpicks.

Step 3

Bake ham in the preheated oven until a meat thermometer inserted into the thickest part of the ham reads 140 degrees F (60 degrees C), 1 1/2 to 2 hours.

Step 4

While the ham is baking, mix the pineapple juice and brown sugar in a microwave-safe ceramic or glass bowl and microwave on medium power until the glaze is boiling and slightly thickened. Work carefully because the glaze will be sticky and very hot.

Step 5

Pour about half the glaze evenly over the ham and pineapple about 1 hour before the end of baking; pour the rest over the ham about 30 minutes before the end of baking.

Cook's Note

A ham baked with this glaze makes excellent leftovers as well, especially the next morning with some more fresh pineapple!

Nutrition Facts

Per Serving:

396.3 calories; protein 23.9g 48% DV; carbohydrates 16.1g 5% DV; fat 25.7g 40% DV; cholesterol 99.4mg 33% DV; sodium 67.7mg 3% DV.

Doughnut in a Mug

Prep: 5 mins **Cook:** 2 mins **Total:** 7 mins **Servings:** 1 **Yield:** 1 doughnut

Ingredients

- 1 egg, beaten
- 2 tablespoons brown sugar
- 2 tablespoons self-rising flour
- 1 ½ tablespoons milk
- 1 tablespoon white sugar
- 1 tablespoon olive oil
- ¼ teaspoon ground cinnamon

Directions

Step 1

Beat egg, brown sugar, self-rising flour, milk, white sugar, olive oil, and cinnamon together in a large mug.

Step 2

Place mug in microwave; cook on high heat for 2 minutes.

Cook's Notes:

Two tablespoons flour and 1/4 teaspoon baking powder can be substituted for the self-raising flour.
Vegetable oil can be substituted for the olive oil, if desired.
If doughnut isn't fully cooked after 2 minutes, microwave for 10 more seconds.

Nutrition Facts

Per Serving:

411 calories; protein 8.7g 17% DV; carbohydrates 52.7g 17% DV; fat 19.1g 29% DV; cholesterol 187.8mg 63% DV; sodium 287.4mg 12% DV.

Microwave Caramel Popcorn

Prep: 5 mins **Cook:** 10 mins **Total:** 15 mins **Servings:** 16 **Yield:** 4 quarts

Ingredients

- 4 quarts popped popcorn
- 1 cup brown sugar
- ½ cup margarine
- ¼ cup light corn syrup
- ½ teaspoon salt
- 1 teaspoon vanilla extract
- ½ teaspoon baking soda

Directions

Step 1

Place the popped popcorn into a large brown paper bag. Set aside.

Step 2

In a 2 quart casserole dish, or other heat-proof glass dish, combine the brown sugar, margarine, corn syrup, salt and vanilla. Heat for 3 minutes in the microwave, then take out and stir until well blended. Return to the microwave, and cook for 1 1/2 minutes. Remove from microwave, and stir in the baking soda.

Step 3

Pour syrup over the popcorn in the bag. Roll down the top once or twice to close the bag, and shake to coat the corn. Place bag into the microwave, and cook for 1 minute and 10 seconds. Remove, shake, flip the bag over, and return it to the microwave. Cook for another 1 minute and 10 seconds. Dump the popcorn out onto waxed paper, and let cool until coating is set. Store in an airtight container.

Nutrition Facts

Per Serving:

172.6 calories; protein 1.1g 2% DV; carbohydrates 23.8g 8% DV; fat 8.7g 13% DV; cholesterolmg; sodium 282mg 11% DV.

Semi-Indulgent Easy Brown Rice

Prep: 10 mins **Cook:** 10 mins **Total:** 20 mins **Servings:** 4 **Yield:** 4 servings

Ingredients

- 1 cup instant brown rice (such as Minute)
- ½ teaspoon dried parsley
- ¼ teaspoon ground black pepper
- 1 tablespoon unsalted butter
- ½ teaspoon lemon juice
- 7 fluid ounces low-sodium chicken broth, or more if needed
-

Directions

Step 1

Combine instant brown rice, parsley, and black pepper in a microwave-safe dish.

Step 2

Place butter and lemon juice in a measuring cup.

Step 3

Pour chicken broth into measuring cup with butter and lemon juice to measure a total of 1 cup.

Step 4

Stir chicken broth mixture into rice mixture until all ingredients are moistened. Cover with microwave-safe lid.

Step 5

Heat in the microwave oven until rice is tender and has absorbed the liquid, about 7 minutes.

Step 6

Remove and let stand for 5 minutes. Fluff with fork before serving.

Cook's note:

You can adjust the seasonings to taste: lime juice and cilantro for a Mexican side, orange juice and thyme for another variety, etc. You can also switch out brown rice for instant white rice or regular-cooking brown rice, but you'll need to read the package to make liquid to dry ratio adjustments.

Nutrition Facts

Per Serving:

109.5 calories; protein 2.5g 5% DV; carbohydrates 16.8g 5% DV; fat 3.6g 6% DV; cholesterol 8.3mg 3% DV; sodium 23.7mg 1% DV.

Soft-Boiled Eggs in the Microwave

Prep: 5 mins **Cook:** 5 mins **Total:** 10 mins **Servings:** 2 **Yield:** 2 eggs

Ingredients

- 1 cup water
- 2 large eggs eggs
- ½ teaspoon salt

Directions

- **Step 1**
  Fill a bowl with warm water and place cold eggs into the bowl, to keep from cracking when you cook them.
- **Step 2**
  Fill a microwave-safe bowl with water; add salt. Microwave on high power to boil, 1 to 1 1/2 minutes.
- **Step 3**
  Place warm eggs into the bowl of hot water and cover the bowl with plastic wrap.
- **Step 4**
  Place the bowl of covered eggs into the microwave and microwave on 60% power for 1 1/2 minutes.
- **Step 5**
  Remove from the microwave and transfer eggs to a bowl of cool water to stop the cooking process. Peel and serve.

Cook's Note:

Cook times may vary some, depending on what microwave is used.

Nutrition Facts

Per Serving:

71.5 calories; protein 6.3g 13% DV; carbohydrates 0.4g; fat 5g 8% DV; cholesterol 186mg 62% DV; sodium 654.9mg 26% DV.

Cinnamon Apples

Prep: 5 mins **Cook:** 2 mins **Total:** 7 mins **Servings:** 4 **Yield:** 4 servings

Ingredients

- 2 eaches apples, diced
- 1 teaspoon white sugar
- ½ teaspoon ground cinnamon

Directions

- **Step 1**
  Place apples in a microwave-safe bowl; heat in microwave for 30 seconds. Sprinkle sugar and cinnamon over apples and stir to coat. Heat apples in microwave until soft and warm, about 1 minute more.

Nutrition Facts

Per Serving:

40.6 calories; protein 0.2g; carbohydrates 10.8g 4% DV; fat 0.1g; cholesterolmg; sodium 0.7mg.

Keto Peanut Butter Fudge Fat Bomb

Prep: 10 mins **Additional:** 2 hrs **Total:** 2 hrs 10 mins **Servings:** 10 **Yield:** 10 servings

Ingredients

- 1 cup unsweetened peanut butter, softened
- 1 cup coconut oil
- ¼ cup unsweetened vanilla-flavored almond milk
- 2 teaspoons vanilla liquid stevia, or as needed

Directions

- **Step 1**
  Line a loaf pan with parchment paper.

- **Step 2**
  Combine peanut butter and coconut oil in a microwave-safe dish. Microwave 30 seconds until slightly melted. Add to blender with almond milk and stevia; blend until well combined. Pour into loaf pan and refrigerate until set, about 2 hours.

Cook's Note:

If you like, you can top the fat bombs with homemade chocolate sauce. Whisk together 1/4 cup unsweetened cocoa powder, 2 tablespoons melted coconut oil, and 2 tablespoons sweetener of choice together until well combined. Drizzle over the fat bomb after it has set.

Nutrition Facts

Per Serving:

341.2 calories; protein 6.5g 13% DV; carbohydrates 5.3g 2% DV; fat 34.9g 54% DV; cholesterolmg; sodium 122.4mg 5% DV.

Keto Cocoa Mug Cake

Prep: 5 mins **Cook:** 1 min **Total:** 6 mins **Servings:** 2 **Yield:** 2 servings

Ingredients

- 6 tablespoons almond flour
- 2 tablespoons unsweetened cocoa powder
- 2 teaspoons low-calorie natural sweetener (such as Swerve)
- ½ teaspoon baking powder
- ⅛ teaspoon salt
- 2 large eggs eggs
- 2 tablespoons coconut oil, melted

Directions

- **Step 1**
  Mix together almond flour, cocoa powder, sweetener, baking powder, and salt in a small bowl.
- **Step 2**
  Beat eggs in a bowl using an electric mixer until light and fluffy. Slowly add melted coconut oil and beaten eggs to the almond flour mixture, whisking everything together with a fork.
- **Step 3**
  Lightly grease 2 microwave-safe mugs. Pour batter into mugs, leaving at least 1 inch of empty space at the top so the cakes can rise.
- **Step 4**
  Microwave on high power for 1 minute. Test cakes for doneness. Continue cooking in 10 second-intervals, if necessary, until cakes are cooked through and not runny in the middle.

Nutrition Facts

Per Serving:

337.8 calories; protein 12.3g 25% DV; carbohydrates 8.6g 3% DV; fat 30.9g 48% DV; cholesterol 186mg 62% DV; sodium 338.4mg 14% DV.

Mocha Truffles

Prep: 30 mins **Cook:** 5 mins **Additional:** 2 hrs **Total:** 2 hrs 35 mins **Servings:** 66 **Yield:** 5 1/2 dozen truffles

Ingredients

Truffle:

- 1 (24 ounce) bag semi-sweet chocolate chips
- 8 ounces cream cheese, softened
- 3 tablespoons instant coffee granules
- 2 teaspoons water

Coating:

- 6 ounces semi-sweet chocolate chips
- 1 tablespoon shortening

Directions

- **Step 1**
  Line a baking sheet with waxed paper.
- **Step 2**
  Melt 24 ounces chocolate chips in a microwave-safe glass or ceramic bowl in 30-second intervals, stirring after each melting, 1 to 3 minutes. Mix cream cheese, coffee granules, and water into melted chocolate until smooth. Chill chocolate mixture until firm enough to shape, about 30 minutes.
- **Step 3**

Shape chocolate mixture into 1-inch balls and place on the prepared baking sheet. Chill truffles until firm, at least 1 to 2 hours.

- **Step 4**
  Melt 6 ounces chocolate chips and shortening in a microwave-safe glass or ceramic bowl in 30-second intervals, stirring after each melting, for 1 to 3 minutes.
- **Step 5**
  Dip truffles in the melted chocolate mixture and return to the waxed paper. Set aside until firm, at least 30 minutes.

Cook's Notes:

White or milk chocolate chips can be used in place of the semi-sweet for the coating.

Nutrition Facts

Per Serving:

75.5 calories; protein 0.9g 2% DV; carbohydrates 8g 3% DV; fat 5.3g 8% DV; cholesterol 3.8mg 1% DV; sodium 11.3mg 1% DV.

Pumpkin Pie Mug Cake

Prep: 5 mins **Cook:** 1 min **Total:** 6 mins **Servings:** 1 **Yield:** 1 serving

Ingredients

- 1 egg
- ¼ cup dark brown sugar
- ⅓ cup all-purpose flour
- ¼ cup canned pumpkin puree
- 1 tablespoon white sugar
- ½ teaspoon vanilla extract
- ½ teaspoon ground cinnamon
- ½ teaspoon ground ginger
- ¼ teaspoon ground nutmeg
- ¼ teaspoon salt

Directions

- **Step 1**
  Crack egg into a microwave-safe mug. Whisk in brown sugar. Add flour, pumpkin puree, white sugar, vanilla extract, cinnamon, ginger, nutmeg, and salt; whisk until well blended.
- **Step 2**
  Cook in the microwave on high until puffed and golden, about 1 minute 15 seconds.

Nutrition Facts

Per Serving:

518.3 calories; protein 11.5g 23% DV; carbohydrates 106g 34% DV; fat 5.9g 9% DV; cholesterol 186mg 62% DV; sodium 816mg 33% DV.

Can't Wait Microwave Lava Cake

Prep: 10 mins **Cook:** 7 mins **Additional:** 5 mins **Total:** 22 mins **Servings:** 4 **Yield:** 4 servings

Ingredients

- 1 serving cooking spray
- 1 (15.25 ounce) package spiced cake mix (such as Betty Crocker)
- 1 cup water
- 3 large eggs eggs
- ⅓ cup vegetable oil
- 1 cup chopped walnuts
- 1 cup semisweet chocolate chips
- 1 (16 ounce) can prepared chocolate frosting
- 1 tablespoon confectioners' sugar

Directions

- **Step 1**
  Grease a microwave-safe bowl or ramekins with nonstick cooking spray.
- **Step 2**
  Combine cake mix, water, eggs, and oil in a large bowl and beat with an electric blender on low speed until moistened, about 30 seconds. Increase to medium speed and beat for 2 minutes. Stir walnuts and chocolate chips into the batter. Pour half of the batter into the prepared microwave safe bowl or ramekins.
- **Step 3**
  Spoon chocolate frosting over the batter and spread evenly over the top. Pour the rest of the batter on top.
- **Step 4**
  Microwave until a toothpick inserted in the middle of the cake comes out clean, 7 minutes for a bowl or 3 to 4 minutes for smaller ramekins. Remove from microwave and let rest, about 5 minutes. Dust with confectioners' sugar.

Cook's Notes:

Moist or pudding cake mixes work best.

You can use any type of nuts besides walnuts.

Nutrition Facts

Per Serving:

1526.2 calories; protein 18.7g 37% DV; carbohydrates 183.4g 59% DV; fat 87g 134% DV; cholesterol 139.5mg 47% DV; sodium 994.2mg 40% DV.

Whole Wheat Cereal Bars

Prep: 5 mins **Cook:** 5 mins **Additional:** 30 mins **Total:** 40 mins **Servings:** 6 **Yield:** 1 - 8 inch square pan

Ingredients

- ½ cup brown sugar
- ½ cup honey
- ½ cup peanut butter
- 3 cups coarsely chopped shredded whole wheat cereal biscuits
- ¾ cup raisins

Directions

- **Step 1**
  Combine brown sugar, honey, and peanut butter in a microwave-safe glass or ceramic bowl. Melt the peanut butter mixture microwave in 30 second intervals, stirring after each melting, for 1 to 2 minutes (depending on your microwave). Stir in cereal and raisins.
- **Step 2**
  Press cereal mixture into an 8 inch square pan sprayed with non-stick spray. Cool and cut into bars.

Nutrition Facts

Per Serving:

412.3 calories; protein 8.4g 17% DV; carbohydrates 77g 25% DV; fat 11.3g 17% DV; cholesterolmg; sodium 109.1mg 4% DV.

Southwest Squash Casserole

Prep: 15 mins **Cook:** 20 mins **Total:** 35 mins **Servings:** 8 **Yield:** 8 Servings

Ingredients

- 2 pounds yellow squash, cut in 1/4 inch slices
- 2 medium (2-1/2" dia)s sweet onions, quartered and separated
- 1 red bell pepper, cut into 1/2 inch pieces
- 1 pound fresh mushrooms, sliced
- 1 (4 ounce) can chopped green chile peppers
- 2 peppers fresh jalapeno peppers, chopped
- 1 (8 ounce) package shredded Monterey Jack cheese
- 1 cup sour cream
- ¾ cup crushed tortilla chips

Directions

- **Step 1**
  Lightly grease a large casserole dish. Arrange the squash, onions, and red bell pepper in the dish. Place in the microwave, and cook on High 10 minutes, stirring once, until tender.

- **Step 2**
  Gently mix the mushrooms, green chile peppers, jalapeno peppers, cheese, and sour cream into the dish. Sprinkle with crushed tortilla chips. Cover dish, and cook in the microwave 10 minutes on Medium-high power, or until cheese is melted and casserole is heated through.

Nutrition Facts

Per Serving:

228.1 calories; protein 11.7g 23% DV; carbohydrates 13.1g 4% DV; fat 15.6g 24% DV; cholesterol 37.6mg 13% DV; sodium 346.6mg 14% DV.

Bangan ka Bhurta (Indian Eggplant)

Prep: 15 mins **Cook:** 15 mins **Additional:** 5 mins **Total:** 35 mins **Servings:** 4 **Yield:** 4 servings

Ingredients

- 1 eggplant
- 1 teaspoon vegetable oil
- 1 medium onion, chopped
- 2 plum tomato (blank)s roma (plum) tomatoes, chopped
- ¼ teaspoon ground cayenne pepper
- ¼ teaspoon salt
- ¼ teaspoon pepper
- 4 sprigs chopped fresh cilantro

Directions

- **Step 1**
  Preheat the oven broiler. Place eggplant in a roasting pan, and broil 5 minutes, turning occasionally, until about 1/2 the skin is scorched.
- **Step 2**
  Place eggplant in microwave safe dish. Cook 5 minutes on High in the microwave, or until tender. Cool enough to handle, and remove skin, leaving some scorched bits. Cut into thick slices.
- **Step 3**
  Heat oil in a skillet over medium heat, stir in the onion, and cook until tender. Mix in eggplant, and tomatoes. Season with cayenne pepper, salt, and black pepper. Continue to cook and stir until soft. Garnish with cilantro to serve.

Nutrition Facts

Per Serving:

60.8 calories; protein 2g 4% DV; carbohydrates 11.8g 4% DV; fat 1.5g 2% DV; cholesterolmg; sodium 152mg 6% DV.

Peachy Oatmeal

Prep: 5 mins **Cook:** 3 mins **Total:** 8 mins **Servings:** 1 **Yield:** 1 serving

Ingredients

- ½ (15 ounce) can sliced peaches, drained
- ½ cup water
- ½ cup milk
- ½ cup quick-cooking oats
- 2 tablespoons packed brown sugar
- ¼ teaspoon ground cinnamon, or more to taste
- 1 pinch salt

Directions

- **Step 1**
  Stir peaches, water, milk, oats, brown sugar, cinnamon, and salt together in a microwave-safe bowl.
- **Step 2**
  Cook in microwave on High, stirring every 60 seconds, until the oats are softened, about 3 minutes. Stir one final time before serving.

Cook's Notes:

I prefer to use 2% milk, but this works just as well with skim milk.
As far as the peaches are concerned, I use the 'no sugar added' variety of sliced peaches.

Nutrition Facts

Per Serving:

411.4 calories; protein 10.7g 22% DV; carbohydrates 84.5g 27% DV; fat 5.1g 8% DV; cholesterol 9.8mg 3% DV; sodium 72.1mg 3% DV.

Microwaved Potatoes Lyonnaise

Prep: 10 mins **Cook:** 10 mins **Total:** 20 mins **Servings:** 6 **Yield:** 6 servings

Ingredients

- 3 large potatoes, peeled and cubed
- 2 small onions, sliced
- 2 tablespoons margarine
- 2 cloves garlic, minced
- ½ teaspoon salt
- ⅛ teaspoon dried oregano
- ⅛ teaspoon black pepper
- ⅛ teaspoon paprika

Directions

- **Step 1**
  In a 3-quart microwave-safe casserole dish, combine potatoes, onions, margarine, garlic, salt, oregano, pepper and paprika.

- **Step 2**
  Heat in microwave on high until margarine melts, about 1 minute; stir. Cook 10 minutes more, stirring occasionally.

Nutrition Facts

Per Serving:

153.8 calories; protein 2.7g 6% DV; carbohydrates 28.3g 9% DV; fat 3.7g 6% DV; cholesterolmg; sodium 525.1mg 21% DV.

Ridiculously Easy Queso Fresco "Dip"

Prep: 10 mins **Cook:** 3 mins **Additional:** 2 hrs **Total:** 2 hrs 13 mins **Servings:** 8 **Yield:** 8 servings

Ingredients

- 1 (12 ounce) package queso fresco
- 1 (16 ounce) jar salsa
- 1 bunch fresh cilantro, chopped
- 1 jalapeno pepper, seeded and diced
- 2 dashes hot pepper sauce (such as Frank's RedHot)

Directions

- **Step 1**
  Slice queso fresco in half horizontally, creating 2 rounds. Transfer to a shallow microwave-safe baking dish.
- **Step 2**
  Spread salsa evenly over queso fresco and pour any residual juices around the dish for the queso fresco to marinate in. Top with cilantro, jalapeno, and hot sauce. Cover with plastic wrap and let marinate, at least 2 hours, preferably longer.
- **Step 3**
  Heat queso fresco in the microwave until slightly softened, about 3 minutes.

Nutrition Facts

Per Serving:

79.1 calories; protein 6.1g 12% DV; carbohydrates 6.2g 2% DV; fat 3.7g 6% DV; cholesterol 13.8mg 5% DV; sodium 401.6mg 16% DV.

Individual Microwave Brownie

Prep: 5 mins **Cook:** 1 min **Total:** 6 mins **Servings:** 1 **Yield:** 1 microwave brownie

Ingredients

- 2 tablespoons all-purpose flour
- 2 tablespoons brown sugar
- 2 tablespoons unsweetened cocoa powder
- ⅛ teaspoon baking powder
- ⅛ teaspoon instant coffee powder
- 1 pinch salt
- 2 tablespoons vegetable oil
- 2 tablespoons water, or as needed
- 2 drops vanilla extract

Directions

- **Step 1**

  Combine flour, sugar, cocoa powder, baking powder, instant coffee, and salt in a microwave-safe mug or small bowl. Mix in vegetable oil, water, and vanilla extract until mixture is smooth and glossy. Add more water, 1/4 teaspoon at a time, if mixture looks a little dry.
- **Step 2**

  Microwave on high until top looks dry, about 1 minute.

Cook's Note:

Using less vegetable oil results in a slightly cakier texture.

Nutrition Facts

Per Serving:

431.2 calories; protein 3.8g 8% DV; carbohydrates 44.8g 15% DV; fat 28.9g 44% DV; cholesterolmg; sodium 227.2mg 9% DV.

Vegan Mug Cake with Pineapple and Mint

Prep: 5 mins **Cook:** 3 mins **Additional:** 5 mins **Total:** 13 mins **Servings:** 2 **Yield:** 2 mug cakes

Ingredients

- 2 slices fresh pineapple
- 1 ripe banana
- 2 tablespoons cream of coconut
- 1 tablespoon rolled oats
- 1 tablespoon quick-cooking oats
- ¼ teaspoon baking powder
- 3 leaves fresh mint
- 1 teaspoon chia seeds
- 1 teaspoon poppy seeds

Directions

- **Step 1**

Combine pineapple, banana, cream of coconut, rolled oats, quick-cooking oats, baking powder, mint, chia seeds, and poppy seeds in a blender; blend until smooth. Pour into 2 mugs.

- **Step 2**
  Microwave at the highest setting until mug cakes have set and risen well, about 3 minutes. Allow to cool a few minutes before serving.

Nutrition Facts

Per Serving:

195.6 calories; protein 2.4g 5% DV; carbohydrates 39.1g 13% DV; fat 4.7g 7% DV; cholesterolmg; sodium 70.1mg 3% DV.

Easy Frozen Hot Chocolate

Prep: 6 mins **Additional:** 5 mins **Total:** 11 mins **Servings:** 4 **Yield:** 4 servings

Ingredients

- 3 ounces semisweet chocolate, chopped
- 2 tablespoons white sugar
- 2 teaspoons unsweetened cocoa powder
- 1 teaspoon vanilla extract
- 1 ½ cups milk, divided
- 3 cups ice

Directions

- **Step 1**
  Microwave chocolate in a small microwave-safe bowl, stirring every 30 seconds until melted, 5 to 7 minutes. Stir in sugar, cocoa powder, and vanilla extract until blended. Whisk in 1/2 cup milk until combined; set aside to cool, about 5 minutes.
- **Step 2**
  Pour chocolate mixture, remaining milk, and ice into a blender; blend on high speed until mixture is creamy, about 1 to 3 minutes.

Cook's Note:

More milk and ice can be added if needed.

Nutrition Facts

Per Serving:

180.2 calories; protein 4.7g 9% DV; carbohydrates 23.2g 8% DV; fat 8.7g 13% DV; cholesterol 7.3mg 2% DV; sodium 37.8mg 2% DV.

Coffee Mug Cake

Prep: 10 mins **Cook:** 1 min **Total:** 11 mins **Servings:** 1 **Yield:** 1 cake

Ingredients

- 1 tablespoon butter, softened

- 2 tablespoons white sugar
- ½ beaten egg
- 2 tablespoons sour cream
- 2 drops vanilla extract, or more to taste
- ¼ cup all-purpose flour
- ⅛ teaspoon baking powder
- 2 tablespoons all-purpose flour
- 1 tablespoon brown sugar
- 1 teaspoon cinnamon
- 1 tablespoon butter

Directions

- **Step 1**
  Stir 1 tablespoon softened butter and white sugar together in a coffee mug until fluffy; stir egg, sour cream, and vanilla extract into the butter mixture. Add 1/4 cup flour and baking powder into the mixture; stir until smooth.
- **Step 2**
  Mix 2 tablespoons flour, brown sugar, and cinnamon together in a bowl. Mash 1 tablespoon butter into the flour mixture with a fork or pastry cutter until mixture is crumbly; sprinkle over the cake batter in the mug.
- **Step 3**
  Cook in microwave oven on high for 1 minute. Continue cooking in 10-second intervals until a toothpick inserted into the middle comes out clean.

Nutrition Facts

Per Serving:

630.9 calories; protein 9.2g 19% DV; carbohydrates 77.7g 25% DV; fat 32g 49% DV; cholesterol 166.7mg 56% DV; sodium 279.9mg 11% DV.

Microwave Pecan Brittle

Prep: 10 mins **Cook:** 9 mins **Additional:** 30 mins **Total:** 49 mins **Servings:** 10 **Yield:** 10 servings

Ingredients

- 1 cup chopped pecans
- 1 cup white sugar
- ½ cup light corn syrup
- ⅛ teaspoon salt
- 1 tablespoon butter
- 1 teaspoon baking soda
- 1 teaspoon vanilla extract

Directions

- **Step 1**
  Butter a baking sheet.
- **Step 2**
  Combine pecans, sugar, corn syrup, and salt in a glass 4-cup measuring cup.
- **Step 3**
  Heat in microwave for 3 1/2 minutes; stir and heat for 3 1/2 more minutes. Stir butter into pecan mixture and heat in microwave for 2 more minutes.
- **Step 4**
  Stir baking soda and vanilla extract into pecan mixture until foamy; pour onto the prepared baking sheet. Allow to cool completely before breaking brittle into pieces. Store in an airtight container.

Nutrition Facts

Per Serving:

217.5 calories; protein 1.1g 2% DV; carbohydrates 34.3g 11% DV; fat 9.7g 15% DV; cholesterol 3.1mg 1% DV; sodium 173.3mg 7% DV.

Easy Butter Fingers Candy

Prep: 10 mins **Cook:** 5 mins **Additional:** 30 mins **Total:** 45 mins **Servings:** 24 **Yield:** 24 pieces

Ingredients

- 1 pound candy corn
- 1 (18 ounce) jar crunchy peanut butter
- 1 (6 ounce) bag semisweet chocolate chips
- 1 tablespoon vegetable shortening, or more if needed

Directions

- **Step 1**
  Line a 9x13-inch pan with parchment paper.
- **Step 2**
  Place candy corn in a microwave-safe bowl (not plastic) and heat in several 30-second intervals, stirring after each interval, until candy corn is warm, melted, and smooth.
- **Step 3**
  Stir peanut butter into melted candy corn until thoroughly combined; transfer candy to the prepared pan, pressing and smoothing the candy into the corners of the pan.
- **Step 4**
  Place chocolate chips and vegetable shortening into the top of a double boiler set over simmering water. Heat the chocolate, stirring constantly, until just warm, melted, and smooth. Spread warm chocolate over the peanut candy. Chill in refrigerator until candy is set, at least 30 minutes, before cutting into squares.

Cook's Notes:

I like to buy candy corn on sale after Halloween to use for making candy for Christmas gifts.

With some store brands of chocolate chips I have had to use 2 tablespoons shortening.

Nutrition Facts

Per Serving:

251.3 calories; protein 6.1g 12% DV; carbohydrates 27.3g 9% DV; fat 14.7g 23% DV; cholesterolmg; sodium 120.4mg 5% DV.

Spanish Rice (Microwave)

Prep: 10 mins **Cook:** 28 mins **Total:** 38 mins **Servings:** 4 **Yield:** 4 servings

Ingredients

- 6 slices bacon, chopped
- 1 cup white rice
- ½ onion, chopped
- 1 (19 ounce) can whole peeled tomatoes
- 1 cup water
- ¼ cup diced green bell pepper
- ¼ cup ketchup
- 1 teaspoon salt
- ½ teaspoon chili powder
- 1 dash ground black pepper

Directions

- **Step 1**
  Place bacon in a microwave-safe 2-quart baking dish. Microwave until crisp, about 6 minutes. Transfer bacon to a plate.
- **Step 2**
  Place rice and onion in the baking dish; microwave until slightly tender, about 4 minutes. Add the cooked bacon, tomatoes, water, green pepper, ketchup, salt, chili powder, and pepper. Cover and microwave for 10 minutes. Stir mixture and continue cooking until rice is tender and flavors are blended, about 8 minutes more. Let cool briefly before serving.

Nutrition Facts

Per Serving:

289.4 calories; protein 10g 20% DV; carbohydrates 48.3g 16% DV; fat 6.4g 10% DV; cholesterol 15.1mg 5% DV; sodium 1264.7mg 51% DV.

Microwave Peanut Butter Chocolate Swirl Fudge

Prep: 10 mins **Cook:** 5 mins **Additional:** 1 hr **Total:** 1 hr 15 mins **Servings:** 60 **Yield:** 60 servings

Ingredients

- 1 (24 ounce) package white almond bark, broken in half
- 12 ounces peanut butter, or more to taste
- 3 (1.5 ounce) bars milk chocolate candy bars (such as Hershey's)

Directions

- **Step 1**
  Line an 8-inch square pan with waxed paper or spray with cooking spray.
- **Step 2**
  Place 1 almond bark half in a microwave-safe bowl; heat in the microwave, in 30-second intervals, stirring after each melting until smooth, 1 to 3 minutes. Add peanut butter to melted almond bark and mix well. Add the remaining almond bark to the bowl and push to the bottom of the bowl.
- **Step 3**
  Heat mixture in the microwave for 1 minute; stir to break up any large pieces. Continue heating in microwave, in 30 second intervals, until completely melted. Pour fudge mixture into the prepared square pan.
- **Step 4**
  Melt chocolate bars in a microwave-safe bowl in 30-second intervals, stirring after each melting, for 1 to 3 minutes. Drizzle melted chocolate over fudge. Swirl the chocolate into the fudge using a knife.
- **Step 5**
  Refrigerate fudge until solid, about 1 hour.

Cook's Note:

If the mixture is refrigerated too long, it is hard to cut and breaks easily. It will soften some if left out at room temperature.

Nutrition Facts

Per Serving:

105.3 calories; protein 2.2g 4% DV; carbohydrates 9.1g 3% DV; fat 7.1g 11% DV; cholesterol 2.9mg 1% DV; sodium 37.2mg 2% DV.

BBQ Potatoes with Green Onions

Prep: 15 mins **Cook:** 30 mins **Additional:** 10 mins **Total:** 55 mins **Servings:** 6 **Yield:** 6 servings

Ingredients

- 6 large potatoes, peeled
- 4 medium (4-1/8" long)s green onions, finely chopped
- 2 tablespoons butter
- salt and ground black pepper to taste

Directions

- **Step 1**
  Preheat an outdoor grill for high heat.
- **Step 2**

Microwave potatoes on High 5 to 8 minutes, until tender but still firm. Cool slightly, and cube.

- **Step 3**
  Place cubed potatoes on a large piece of foil. Top with green onions. Dot with butter, and season with salt and pepper. Tightly seal foil around the potatoes.
- **Step 4**
  Cook on the prepared grill 20 to 30 minutes, until tender.

Nutrition Facts

Per Serving:

321.3 calories; protein 7.7g 15% DV; carbohydrates 65.2g 21% DV; fat 4.2g 6% DV; cholesterol 10.2mg 3% DV; sodium 51mg 2% DV.

S'mores Rice Crispy Treats

Prep: 10 mins **Cook:** 10 mins **Additional:** 15 mins **Total:** 35 mins **Servings:** 16 **Yield:** 16 treats

Ingredients

- 4 cups crispy rice cereal
- 2 cups honey graham cereal (such as Golden Grahams)
- 4 tablespoons butter
- 1 (10.5 ounce) package large marshmallows (such as Jet-Puffed)
- 4 (1.5 ounce) milk chocolate bars (such as Hershey's)

Directions

- **Step 1**
  Grease a 9x11-inch pan. Mix rice cereal and honey graham cereal together in a large bowl; set aside.
- **Step 2**
  Melt butter over medium heat in a large saucepan. Stir in marshmallows until completely melted and combined with butter, 5 to 7 minutes. Remove from heat. Stir in cereal mixture until coated. Pour into the prepared pan and gently compress with a greased spatula.
- **Step 3**
  Melt chocolate in a microwave-safe bowl in a microwave oven, heating and mixing until chocolate is melted, in 30-second increments. Spread chocolate over cereal mixture and allow to cool completely, 15 to 30 minutes. Cut and serve.

Nutrition Facts

Per Serving:

186.2 calories; protein 1.8g 4% DV; carbohydrates 31.6g 10% DV; fat 6.3g 10% DV; cholesterol 10.1mg 3% DV; sodium 142mg 6% DV.

Jicama Zebra Fries

Prep: 10 mins **Cook:** 10 mins **Total:** 20 mins **Servings:** 2 **Yield:** 2 servings

Ingredients

- 1 serving cooking spray
- 1 cup French fry-sized pieces of jicama

Directions

- **Step 1**

  Spray a microwave-safe plate with cooking spray. Arrange jicama pieces on plate.
- **Step 2**

  Cook in the microwave on high until small brown stripes begin to form on the fries, 9 to 11 minutes. Check on the fries every few minutes to avoid burning. Remove plate from microwave with an oven mitt because plate will be hot.

Nutrition Facts

Per Serving:

25.9 calories; protein 0.5g 1% DV; carbohydrates 5.7g 2% DV; fat 0.2g; cholesterolmg; sodium 2.6mg.

Quick Peach Cobbler In a Mug

Prep: 5 mins **Cook:** 2 mins **Additional:** 1 min **Total:** 8 mins **Servings:** 1 **Yield:** 1 serving

Ingredients

- 1 tablespoon butter
- 2 tablespoons water
- 2 tablespoons all-purpose flour
- 1 tablespoon non-fat dry milk
- ⅛ teaspoon baking powder
- ⅛ teaspoon ground cinnamon
- 1 pinch salt
- 1 (4 ounce) container sliced peaches, well drained

Directions

- **Step 1**

  Melt butter in a mug in microwave, about 20 seconds.
- **Step 2**

  Stir water, flour, dry milk, baking powder, ground cinnamon, and salt into butter until well blended. Place peach slices on top of batter.
- **Step 3**

  Microwave on 70% power until cooked through, about 2 minutes. Let stand in microwave for 1 minute to set.

Nutrition Facts

Per Serving:

235.8 calories; protein 5.1g 10% DV; carbohydrates 29.1g 9% DV; fat 11.8g 18% DV; cholesterol 32mg 11% DV; sodium 343.1mg 14% DV.

Easy Turkish Delight

Prep: 20 mins **Cook:** 20 mins **Additional:** 30 mins **Total:** 1 hr 10 mins **Servings:** 35 **Yield:** 35 servings

Ingredients

- 3 cups water
- 2 cups white sugar
- ¼ cup unflavored gelatin
- 1 ½ cups confectioners' sugar, sifted
- ⅔ cup corn flour
- ¼ teaspoon cream of tartar
- ½ teaspoon rose water
- 3 drops pink food coloring, or as desired
- ¾ cup confectioners' sugar, sifted

Directions

- **Step 1**
  Combine water, white sugar, and gelatin in a large microwave-safe bowl; heat in microwave on high for 7 minutes. Stir sugar mixture and cook in microwave for 7 minutes more.
- **Step 2**
  Mix 1 1/2 cups confectioners' sugar, corn flour, and cream of tartar together in a bowl; stir into sugar mixture. Heat mixture in microwave on high for 6 minutes more. Stir rose water and food coloring into mixture.
- **Step 3**
  Lightly grease a 7x11-inch baking dish. Pour mixture into the greased dish; refrigerate until firm, about 30 minutes.
- **Step 4**
  Cut Turkish delight into small squares using a wet knife.
- **Step 5**
  Place 3/4 cup confectioners' sugar in a bowl. Roll Turkish delight in the confectioners' sugar until evenly coated. Store in an airtight container in the refrigerator.

Nutrition Facts

Per Serving:

87.1 calories; protein 0.8g 2% DV; carbohydrates 21.5g 7% DV; fatg; cholesterolmg; sodium 2.2mg.

Vegan Mug Cake

Prep: 5 mins **Cook:** 3 mins **Total:** 8 mins **Servings:** 1 **Yield:** 1 mug cake

Ingredients

- 4 tablespoons all-purpose flour
- 3 tablespoons white sugar
- 2 tablespoons unsweetened cocoa powder
- ¼ teaspoon baking powder
- 4 tablespoons applesauce
- 3 tablespoons soy milk
- 1 tablespoon vegan chocolate chips, or more to taste
- 1 tablespoon toasted flaked coconut

Directions

- **Step 1**
  Combine flour, sugar, cocoa powder, and baking powder in a mug. Stir applesauce and soy milk together in a bowl and add to flour mixture. Stir until well combined. Fold in chocolate chips and sprinkle with coconut.
- **Step 2**
  Microwave at the highest setting until mug cake has set and risen well, about 3 minutes.

Nutrition Facts

Per Serving:

448.8 calories; protein 8.4g 17% DV; carbohydrates 87.2g 28% DV; fat 12.8g 20% DV; cholesterolmg; sodium 151.8mg 6% DV.

Lazy Green Peas

Prep: 5 mins **Cook:** 3 mins **Total:** 8 mins **Servings:** 2 **Yield:** 1 cup

Ingredients

- 1 cup frozen peas
- 1 tablespoon shredded Italian cheese blend (such as Wegmans)
- 1 teaspoon nutritional yeast, or more to taste
- 1 pinch garlic powder, or to taste
- 1 pinch salt and ground black pepper to taste

Directions

- **Step 1**
  Heat frozen peas in a small microwave-safe bowl on high in the microwave until hot, about 3 minutes.
- **Step 2**
  Stir Italian cheese blend, nutritional yeast, and garlic powder into peas; season with salt and black pepper.

Nutrition Facts

Per Serving:

76.5 calories; protein 5.5g 11% DV; carbohydrates 11.3g 4% DV; fat 1.3g 2% DV; cholesterol 2.8mg 1% DV; sodium 193.3mg 8% DV.

Paleo One-Minute MuffinPeanut Butter Popcorn

Prep: 10 mins **Cook:** 5 mins **Total:** 15 mins **Servings:** 8 **Yield:** 8 servings

Ingredients

- 2 (3.5 ounce) packages microwave popcorn, popped
- ½ cup margarine
- ¾ cup brown sugar
- ¼ cup peanut butter
- 20 regulars large marshmallows

Directions

- **Step 1**

  Pour popcorn into a large bowl. In a glass or plastic bowl, combine the margarine, brown sugar, and marshmallows. Cook at 1 minute intervals in the microwave, stirring between each time, until the mixture is melted and smooth. Stir in the peanut butter until well blended. Pour the melted mixture over the popcorn, and stir quickly to coat the corn before it cools.

Nutrition Facts

Per Serving:

380.5 calories; protein 4.7g 9% DV; carbohydrates 43.9g 14% DV; fat 22.3g 34% DV; cholesterolmg; sodium 405.8mg 16% DV.

Minute Chocolate Mug Cake

Prep: 10 mins **Cook:** 2 mins **Additional:** 5 mins **Total:** 17 mins **Servings:** 2 **Yield:** 2 servings

Ingredients

- 1 large egg
- ¼ cup white sugar
- 1 pinch salt
- 2 tablespoons unsweetened cocoa powder
- 2 tablespoons butter, melted
- 1 tablespoon vegetable oil
- ⅛ teaspoon vanilla extract
- 1 tablespoon unsweetened shredded coconut
- 2 tablespoons toasted sliced almonds
- 1 ½ tablespoons miniature semisweet chocolate chips
- 3 tablespoons milk

- ¼ cup all-purpose flour
- ¼ teaspoon baking powder
- ¼ teaspoon confectioners' sugar
- ¼ teaspoon unsweetened cocoa powder, or as needed

Directions

- **Step 1**
- Whisk egg, sugar, salt, 2 tablespoons cocoa powder, butter, vegetable oil, and vanilla extract together in a bowl until smooth. Stir coconut, almonds, and chocolate chips into the mixture; whisk in milk.
- **Step 2**
  Place flour into a small bowl or measuring cup and stir baking powder into flour with a mini whisk or fork. Pour flour mixture over batter and whisk just until you can't see visible flour.
- **Step 3**
- Divide batter evenly between 2 coffee cups. Gently tap the cups on a work surface to eliminate air bubbles.
- **Step 4**
- Place cups into microwave oven, one at a time. Microwave each cup on High for 45 seconds. Nothing will happen in the first 30 seconds; in the last 10 to 15 seconds, batter will begin to rise in the cup. Cooked cake will collapse after microwaving. Remove from oven and let cool 2 to 3 minutes.
- **Step 5**
- Lightly dust each serving with confectioners' sugar and 1/8 teaspoon cocoa. Place each coffee cup onto a saucer and serve.

Cook's Note:

To toast sliced almonds, place them into a dry skillet over medium heat and shake the skillet constantly until almonds are golden brown and fragrant, 1 to 2 minutes. Remove from skillet and let cool.

Nutrition Facts

Per Serving:

471.7 calories; protein 8.5g 17% DV; carbohydrates 48.7g 16% DV; fat 29.5g 45% DV; cholesterol 125.4mg 42% DV; sodium 190.6mg 8% DV.

Blueberry, Coconut, and Pistachio Chocolate Bark

Prep: 10 mins **Cook:** 2 mins **Additional:** 45 mins **Total:** 57 mins **Servings:** 8 **Yield:** 8 servings

Ingredients

- 3 (4 ounce) bars dark chocolate, chopped, divided
- 3 tablespoons shelled unsalted pistachios, coarsely chopped

- 3 tablespoons dried blueberries
- 1 tablespoon coconut chips
- 2 teaspoons grated orange zest

Directions

- **Step 1**
  Melt 8 ounces chocolate in a microwave-safe glass or ceramic bowl in 15-second intervals, stirring after each melting, 1 to 3 minutes. Once chocolate is nearly melted, but a few chunks remain, stop microwaving and stir until completely smooth. Add the remaining 4 ounces of unmelted chocolate. Stir well until all the chocolate has melted.

- **Step 2**
  Lay out a large sheet of parchment paper on a flat work surface. Pour melted chocolate onto parchment and spread chocolate into a thin, even layer using a spatula. Scatter pistachios, dried blueberries, coconut chips, and orange zest quickly over chocolate before it sets.
- **Step 3**
  Leave the chocolate to set fully, about 45 minutes. Break into randomly sized pieces and store in an airtight container.

Cook's Notes:

Use a good quality dark chocolate with at least 60% cacao for best results.

Adding the unmelted chocolate tempers the mixture, and along with stirring results in a glossier finish.

Nutrition Facts

Per Serving:

254.8 calories; protein 3.1g 6% DV; carbohydrates 28.6g 9% DV; fat 15.5g 24% DV; cholesterol 2.1mg 1% DV; sodium 4.2mg.

Microwave Apple Kugel

Prep: 15 mins **Cook:** 15 mins **Total:** 30 mins **Servings:** 9 **Yield:** 1 8-inch square dish

Ingredients

- 1 (8 ounce) package egg noodles
- 3 eaches eggs
- ⅓ cup white sugar
- 2 eaches apples - peeled, cored and finely chopped
- ½ cup sour cream
- ½ cup cottage cheese
- 1 teaspoon ground cinnamon
- ½ teaspoon salt
- ⅓ cup raisins

- 2 tablespoons brown sugar
- 2 tablespoons chopped walnuts
- 2 tablespoons butter

Directions

- **Step 1**
  Fill a large pot with lightly salted water and bring to a rolling boil over high heat. Once the water is boiling, stir in the egg noodles, and return to a boil. Cook the pasta uncovered, stirring occasionally, until the pasta has cooked through, but is still firm to the bite, about 5 minutes. Drain well in a colander set in the sink.
- **Step 2**
  Grease an 8-inch square microwave-safe glass baking dish. Beat the eggs together in a mixing bowl. Stir in the cooked noodles, white sugar, chopped apples, sour cream, cottage cheese, cinnamon, salt, and raisins; mix until combined. Pour the mixture into the prepared dish.
- **Step 3**
  Microwave on medium high (70% power) for 7 minutes.
- **Step 4**
  Combine the brown sugar and chopped walnuts in a bowl, and cut in the butter to form a crumbly topping. Sprinkle the topping over the pudding. Return the pudding to the microwave and cook on medium high (70% power) until the pudding is firm in the center, 7 to 9 minutes.

Nutrition Facts

Per Serving:

265.1 calories; protein 7.9g 16% DV; carbohydrates 38.6g 13% DV; fat 9.5g 15% DV; cholesterol 89.7mg 30% DV; sodium 232.4mg 9% DV.

Microwave Baked Apples

Prep: 7 mins **Cook:** 4 mins **Total:** 11 mins **Servings:** 2 **Yield:** 2 servings

Ingredients

- 2 medium (2-3/4" dia) (approx 3 per lb)s apples
- 2 tablespoons brown sugar
- 1 teaspoon ground nutmeg
- 1 teaspoon ground cinnamon
- 2 teaspoons butter

Directions

- **Step 1**
  Core the apples, leaving the bottom intact.

- **Step 2**
  In a bowl, mix the brown sugar, cinnamon and nutmeg. Spoon the sugar mixture into the apples and set a teaspoon (or more to your taste) of butter on top of each apple. Place the apples in a deep casserole dish and cover.
- **Step 3**
  Microwave for 3 1/2 to 4 minutes or until tender. Let the apples sit for a couple minutes before serving.

Nutrition Facts

Per Serving:

185.7 calories; protein 0.5g 1% DV; carbohydrates 37.6g 12% DV; fat 5.1g 8% DV; cholesterol 10.8mg 4% DV; sodium 33mg 1% DV.

Mocha Truffles

Prep: 30 mins **Cook:** 5 mins **Additional:** 2 hrs **Total:** 2 hrs 35 mins **Servings:** 66 **Yield:** 5 1/2 dozen truffles

Ingredients

Truffle:

- 1 (24 ounce) bag semi-sweet chocolate chips
- 8 ounces cream cheese, softened
- 3 tablespoons instant coffee granules
- 2 teaspoons water

Coating:

- 6 ounces semi-sweet chocolate chips
- 1 tablespoon shortening

Directions

- **Step 1**
  Line a baking sheet with waxed paper.
- **Step 2**
  Melt 24 ounces chocolate chips in a microwave-safe glass or ceramic bowl in 30-second intervals, stirring after each melting, 1 to 3 minutes. Mix cream cheese, coffee granules, and water into melted chocolate until smooth. Chill chocolate mixture until firm enough to shape, about 30 minutes.
- **Step 3**
  Shape chocolate mixture into 1-inch balls and place on the prepared baking sheet. Chill truffles until firm, at least 1 to 2 hours.
- **Step 4**
  Melt 6 ounces chocolate chips and shortening in a microwave-safe glass or ceramic bowl in 30-second intervals, stirring after each melting, for 1 to 3 minutes.

- **Step 5**
  Dip truffles in the melted chocolate mixture and return to the waxed paper. Set aside until firm, at least 30 minutes.

Cook's Notes:

White or milk chocolate chips can be used in place of the semi-sweet for the coating.

Nutrition Facts

Per Serving:

75.5 calories; protein 0.9g 2% DV; carbohydrates 8g 3% DV; fat 5.3g 8% DV; cholesterol 3.8mg 1% DV; sodium 11.3mg 1% DV.

PB and J Mini Mug Cakes

Prep: 10 mins **Cook:** 5 mins **Total:** 15 mins **Servings:** 4 **Yield:** 4 mug cakes

Ingredients

- 4 servings cooking spray (such as Pam)
- 4 teaspoons Concord grape jelly
- ½ cup yellow cake mix
- 2 tablespoons creamy peanut butter (such as Peter Pan)
- 2 cups whipped cream (such as Reddi-Whip)
- ¼ cup egg substitute (such as Egg Beaters)

Directions

- **Step 1**
  Spray the insides of 4 microwave-safe mugs with cooking spray.
- **Step 2**
  Spoon 1 teaspoon grape jelly into the bottom of each mug.
- **Step 3**
  Whisk cake mix and peanut butter together in a bowl; add whipped cream and egg substitute and whisk until batter is smooth. Divide batter evenly between the mugs.
- **Step 4**
  Place 1 mug in the microwave and cook on high until cake is set, about 1 minute, 15 seconds. Repeat with remaining mugs. Invert each mug onto a plate to release cakes.

Nutrition Facts

Per Serving:

230 calories; protein 5.6g 11% DV; carbohydrates 22.9g 7% DV; fat 13.5g 21% DV; cholesterol 23.3mg 8% DV; sodium 215mg 9% DV.

Fudgy Nutella Mug Cake

Prep: 5 mins **Cook:** 2 mins **Additional:** 5 mins **Total:** 12 mins **Servings:** 1 **Yield:** 1 serving

Ingredients

- 2 tablespoons all-purpose flour
- 2 tablespoons coconut flour
- 1 tablespoon cocoa powder
- ¼ teaspoon baking powder
- 3 ½ tablespoons almond milk, divided
- ½ teaspoon vanilla extract
- 3 tablespoons chocolate-hazelnut spread (such as Nutella)

Directions

- **Step 1**
  Stir all-purpose flour, coconut flour, cocoa powder and baking powder together in a small bowl; add 3 tablespoons almond milk, vanilla extract, Nutella and 1/2 tablespoon milk, respectively, stirring between each addition until you finally have a smooth batter. Transfer batter to mug.
- **Step 2**
  Cook in microwave for 1 minute. Allow to rest for about 5 seconds and continue cooking until a toothpick inserted in the center comes out clean, about 30 seconds more.
- **Step 3**
  Let cake cool for 2 to 4 minutes.

Cook's Note:

You can subsitiute 7/8 tablespoon whole wheat flour for the all-purpose flour.

Nutrition Facts

Per Serving:

330 calories; protein 5.9g 12% DV; carbohydrates 45.8g 15% DV; fat 15g 23% DV; cholesterolmg; sodium 203.4mg 8% DV.

Shorecook's Cashew Brittle

Prep: 10 mins **Cook:** 10 mins **Additional:** 30 mins **Total:** 50 mins **Servings:** 15 **Yield:** 15 servings

Ingredients

- 1 tablespoon butter
- 1 ½ cups salted cashews
- 1 cup white sugar
- ½ cup light corn syrup
- 1 tablespoon butter

- 1 teaspoon vanilla extract
- 1 teaspoon baking soda

Directions

- **Step 1**
  Grease a baking sheet with 1 tablespoon butter.
- **Step 2**
  Combine cashews, sugar, and corn syrup in a large microwave-safe glass or ceramic bowl. Microwave on high until sugar melts and mixture is hot, about 6 1/2 minutes.
- **Step 3**
  Stir 1 tablespoon butter and vanilla extract into cashew mixture. Microwave until hot, about 2 1/2 minutes more. Stir baking soda into cashew mixture until light and foamy. Spread mixture on prepared baking sheet. Cool completely and break into pieces.

Cook's Note:

To make it easier to spread, keep your buttered cookie sheet in a warm oven (heat the oven and turn it off). Also, use a buttered silicone spatula for spreading. You do not have to cover the whole cookie sheet. Tilt the sheet and it will also start to spread.

Nutrition Facts

Per Serving:

175.6 calories; protein 2.1g 4% DV; carbohydrates 26.2g 9% DV; fat 7.9g 12% DV; cholesterol 4.1mg 1% DV; sodium 189.3mg 8% DV.

Individual Microwave Brownie

Prep: 5 mins **Cook:** 1 min **Total:** 6 mins **Servings:** 1 **Yield:** 1 microwave brownie

Ingredients

- 2 tablespoons all-purpose flour
- 2 tablespoons brown sugar
- 2 tablespoons unsweetened cocoa powder
- ⅛ teaspoon baking powder
- ⅛ teaspoon instant coffee powder
- 1 pinch salt
- 2 tablespoons vegetable oil
- 2 tablespoons water, or as needed
- 2 drops vanilla extract

Directions

- **Step 1**

Combine flour, sugar, cocoa powder, baking powder, instant coffee, and salt in a microwave-safe mug or small bowl. Mix in vegetable oil, water, and vanilla extract until mixture is smooth and glossy. Add more water, 1/4 teaspoon at a time, if mixture looks a little dry.

- **Step 2**
  Microwave on high until top looks dry, about 1 minute.

Cook's Note:

Using less vegetable oil results in a slightly cakier texture.

Nutrition Facts

Per Serving:

431.2 calories; protein 3.8g 8% DV; carbohydrates 44.8g 15% DV; fat 28.9g 44% DV; cholesterolmg; sodium 227.2mg 9% DV.

Microwave Apple Crisp

Prep: 15 mins **Cook:** 12 mins **Total:** 27 mins **Servings:** 6 **Yield:** 6 servings

Ingredients

- 4 large Granny Smith apples - peeled, cored and sliced
- ½ cup butter, melted
- ¾ cup packed brown sugar
- ¾ cup quick cooking oats
- ½ cup all-purpose flour
- 1 teaspoon ground cinnamon
- ½ teaspoon allspice

Directions

- **Step 1**
  Spread the apples evenly in an 8 inch square glass baking dish. A deep dish glass pie plate will also work. In a medium bowl, mix together the melted butter, brown sugar, oats, flour, cinnamon and allspice. Sprinkle this topping evenly over the apples.
- **Step 2**
  Cook on full power in the microwave for 10 to 12 minutes, until apples can easily be pierced with a knife. Enjoy!

Nutrition Facts

Per Serving:

381.7 calories; protein 3.1g 6% DV; carbohydrates 60.1g 19% DV; fat 16.1g 25% DV; cholesterol 40.7mg 14% DV; sodium 119.2mg 5% DV.

No-Egg Blueberry Mug Cake

Prep: 5 mins **Cook:** 2 mins **Total:** 7 mins **Servings:** 1 **Yield:** 1 serving

Ingredients

- 4 tablespoons all-purpose flour
- 3 tablespoons white sugar
- 1 teaspoon vanilla sugar
- 1 pinch baking powder
- 3 tablespoons milk
- ½ tablespoon olive oil
- 10 eaches blueberries
- 1 teaspoon confectioners' sugar

Directions

- **Step 1**
  Combine flour, sugar, vanilla sugar, and baking powder in a large mug. Add milk and oil; mix batter well with a fork or a small whisk. Carefully fold in blueberries so they are completely covered with batter.
- **Step 2**
  Microwave on high until cake has risen by 50%, 30 seconds to 2 minutes, depending on strength of your microwave. Allow to cool in the mug for a few minutes. Dust with confectioners' sugar.

Cook's Note:

You can substitute the vanilla sugar with 1/4 teaspoon of vanilla extract plus 1 teaspoon of sugar.

Nutrition Facts

Per Serving:

375.7 calories; protein 4.8g 10% DV; carbohydrates 72.4g 23% DV; fat 8g 12% DV; cholesterol 3.7mg 1% DV; sodium 125.7mg 5% DV.

Microwave Scalloped Potatoes

Prep: 10 mins **Cook:** 15 mins **Total:** 25 mins **Servings:** 6 **Yield:** 6 servings

Ingredients

- 4 medium (2-1/4" to 3" dia, raw)s potatoes, peeled and sliced
- ½ cup chopped onion
- 2 tablespoons butter
- 2 tablespoons all-purpose flour
- 2 teaspoons salt

- 1 ½ cups milk
- ½ teaspoon dried parsley, or to taste
- 1 pinch ground paprika, or to taste

Directions

- **Step 1**
  Place potatoes, onion, and butter in a large microwave-safe dish.
- **Step 2**
  Mix flour and salt in a bowl; sprinkle over potatoes and gently toss until vegetables are coated.
- **Step 3**
  Pour milk over the potatoes.
- **Step 4**
  Cook in the microwave on high setting until potatoes are tender, about 15 minutes, stirring every 5 minutes.
- **Step 5**
  Allow potatoes to rest for 5 minutes before sprinkling with parsley and paprika for serving.

Nutrition Facts

Per Serving:

189.2 calories; protein 5.4g 11% DV; carbohydrates 31g 10% DV; fat 5.2g 8% DV; cholesterol 15.1mg 5% DV; sodium 836.8mg 34% DV

Prep: 5 mins **Cook:** 1 min **Total:** 6 mins **Servings:** 1 **Yield:** 2 muffins

Ingredients

- ¼ cup almond flour
- 2 tablespoons flax seed meal
- 1 large egg
- ½ teaspoon coconut oil
- ½ teaspoon ground cinnamon
- ¼ teaspoon baking powder, or as needed
- 1 pinch salt

Directions

- **Step 1**
  Lightly grease 2 microwave-safe ramekins.
- **Step 2**
  Stir almond flour, flax meal, egg, coconut oil, cinnamon, baking powder, and salt in a bowl. Divide almond mixture between ramekins.
- **Step 3**

Heat ramekins in the microwave for 30 seconds; let rest 5 seconds. Heat ramekins for an additional 30 seconds until muffins are risen and cooked. Remove from microwave and flip upside-down onto a plate to cool.

Nutrition Facts

Per Serving:

285 calories; protein 20.1g 40% DV; carbohydrates 13.8g 5% DV; fat 18.4g 28% DV; cholesterol 186mg 62% DV; sodium 353.2mg 14% DV.

Beets with Mandarin Oranges

Prep: 10 mins **Cook:** 5 mins **Total:** 15 mins **Servings:** 5 **Yield:** 5 servings

Ingredients

- ¼ cup white sugar
- ¼ cup apple cider vinegar
- ½ teaspoon apple pie spice
- 2 tablespoons cornstarch
- 1 (15 ounce) can sliced beets, drained
- 1 (15 ounce) can mandarin orange segments, drained

Directions

- **Step 1**
  Whisk together sugar, vinegar, apple pie spice, and cornstarch in a large, microwave safe bowl until combined.
- **Step 2**
  Cook in microwave on High until the mixture is boiling and has thickened, stirring occasionally, about 2 minutes. Stir the drained beets and mandarin orange segments into the thickened sauce. Allow the beets to reheat in the sauce, do not microwave further, or the mandarin oranges will come apart. Serve either warm or cold.

Nutrition Facts

Per Serving:

111.3 calories; protein 1.3g 3% DV; carbohydrates 27.3g 9% DV; fat 0.1g; cholesterolmg; sodium 170.1mg 7% DV.

Taco Lasagna with Noodles

Prep: 10 mins **Cook:** 10 mins **Additional:** 5 mins **Total:** 25 mins **Servings:** 9 **Yield:** 8 to 10 servings

Ingredients

- 11 ounces lasagna noodles

- 1 pound lean ground beef
- 24 ounces tomato sauce
- ½ cup water
- 1 (1 ounce) package taco seasoning mix
- 8 cups shredded Cheddar cheese
- ½ cup crushed tortilla chips

Directions

- **Step 1**
  Bring a large pot of lightly salted water to a boil. Add pasta and cook for 8 to 10 minutes or until al dente; drain.
- **Step 2**
  Meanwhile, in a large skillet, brown beef over medium heat until no longer pink; drain. Add tomato sauce, water and taco seasoning. Lower heat and simmer for 5 minutes.
- **Step 3**
  In a 9x13 inch glass baking dish, layer noodles then meat mixture and cheese; repeat 2 more times. There will be 3 layers.
- **Step 4**
  Cover with plastic wrap and microwave for 10 minutes. Remove from microwave, uncover and let stand for 5 minutes.
- **Step 5**
  Sprinkle tortilla chips over the top; serve.

Nutrition Facts

Per Serving:

709 calories; protein 39.3g 79% DV; carbohydrates 35.8g 12% DV; fat 45.4g 70% DV; cholesterol 143.3mg 48% DV; sodium 1304.5mg 52% DV.

Chocolate Marshmallow Fondant

Prep: 20 mins **Cook:** 2 mins **Additional:** 8 hrs **Total:** 8 hrs 22 mins **Servings:** 10 **Yield:** 10 servings

Ingredients

- 1 (16 ounce) package miniature marshmallows
- 2 tablespoons light corn syrup, or more to taste
- 1 teaspoon coffee-flavored extract
- ½ cup chocolate chips, or more to taste
- 4 cups confectioners' sugar, or more to taste

Directions

- **Step 1**

Melt marshmallows in a large microwave-safe bowl in 30-second intervals, stirring after each melting, 1 to 2 minutes. Mix in light corn syrup and coffee-flavored extract.

- **Step 2**
  Melt chocolate chips in a microwave-safe bowl in 30-second intervals, stirring after each melting, 1 to 2 minutes. Fold into the marshmallow mixture.
- **Step 3**
  Stir confectioners' sugar into the chocolate-marshmallow mixture, 1 cup at a time, until a thick, stringy dough forms.
- **Step 4**
  Dust a flat work surface with confectioners' sugar; turn dough out and knead until smooth and no longer sticky. Wrap tightly in plastic wrap. Let fondant rest at room temperature, 8 hours to overnight.
- **Step 5**
  Dust a flat work surface with confectioners' sugar and roll out fondant to desired size.

Cook's Notes:

You can use milk, semisweet, or dark chocolate chips.

Brown food coloring may be added in step 1 to achieve desired "chocolate" hue.

Nutrition Facts

Per Serving:

409.4 calories; protein 0.4g 1% DV; carbohydrates 95.2g 31% DV; fat 2.6g 4% DV; cholesterolmg; sodium 60mg 2% DV.

Easy Microwave Maple Fudge

Prep: 10 mins **Cook:** 3 mins **Additional:** 15 mins **Total:** 28 mins **Servings:** 64 **Yield:** 64 1x1 inch pieces

Ingredients

- 1 (16 ounce) package confectioners' sugar
- 3 tablespoons milk
- 1 tablespoon maple extract
- ½ cup butter
- ¾ cup chopped walnuts

Directions

- **Step 1**
  Line a baking dish with plastic wrap.
- **Step 2**
  Sift the confectioners' sugar into a large, microwave-safe bowl. Add the milk, maple extract, and butter to the bowl, but do not stir.
- **Step 3**

Heat in microwave on full power for 3 minutes.

- **Step 4**
  Stir the walnuts into the fudge mixture until the fudge begins to thicken; pour into the lined baking dish. Smooth the top of the fudge with a spatula. Refrigerate until firm, about 15 minutes. Remove the fudge from the pan using the plastic wrap as a handle. Cut into small squares and store in an airtight container.

Nutrition Facts

Per Serving:

50.1 calories; protein 0.3g 1% DV; carbohydrates 7.2g 2% DV; fat 2.4g 4% DV; cholesterol 3.9mg 1% DV; sodium 10.6mg.

Chili Cheese Dip V

Prep: 10 mins **Cook:** 5 mins **Total:** 15 mins **Servings:** 32 **Yield:** 4 cups

Ingredients

- 1 (8 ounce) package cream cheese, softened
- 1 (15 ounce) can chili
- 1 cup shredded Cheddar cheese

Directions

- **Step 1**
  In the bottom of a 9 inch, microwave safe round baking dish, spread the cream cheese. Top cream cheese with an even layer of chili. Sprinkle Cheddar cheese over the chili.
- **Step 2**
  Heat in the microwave on high heat 5 minutes, or until the cheese has melted.

Nutrition Facts

Per Serving:

53.4 calories; protein 2.2g 4% DV; carbohydrates 1.8g 1% DV; fat 4.3g 7% DV; cholesterol 13.6mg 5% DV; sodium 111.2mg 4% DV.

Hasty Chocolate Pudding

Prep: 5 mins **Cook:** 10 mins **Total:** 15 mins **Servings:** 4 **Yield:** 4 servings

Ingredients

- ½ cup white sugar
- ⅓ cup unsweetened cocoa powder
- 3 tablespoons cornstarch
- 2 cups milk
- 2 teaspoons vanilla extract

Directions

- **Step 1**
  In a microwave-safe bowl, whisk together the sugar, cocoa and cornstarch. Whisk in milk a little at a time so the mixture does not have any dry lumps.
- **Step 2**
  Place in the microwave, and cook for 3 minutes on high. Stir, then cook at 1 minute intervals, stirring between cooking times for 2 to 4 minutes, or until shiny and thick. Stir in vanilla.
- **Step 3**
  Place a piece of plastic wrap directly on the surface of the pudding to prevent a skin from forming, and chill in the refrigerator. Serve cold.

Nutrition Facts

Per Serving:

203.3 calories; protein 5.4g 11% DV; carbohydrates 40.3g 13% DV; fat 3.4g 5% DV; cholesterol 9.8mg 3% DV; sodium 52.3mg 2% DV.

Potato Chips

Prep: 30 mins **Cook:** 5 mins **Total:** 35 mins **Servings:** 4 **Yield:** 4 servings

Ingredients

- 1 tablespoon vegetable oil
- 1 potato, sliced paper thin (peel optional)
- ½ teaspoon salt, or to taste

Directions

- **Step 1**
  Pour the vegetable oil into a plastic bag (a produce bag works well). Add the potato slices, and shake to coat.
- **Step 2**
  Coat a large dinner plate lightly with oil or cooking spray. Arrange potato slices in a single layer on the dish.
- **Step 3**
  Cook in the microwave for 3 to 5 minutes, or until lightly browned (if not browned, they will not become crisp). Times will vary depending on the power of your microwave. Remove chips from plate, and toss with salt (or other seasonings). Let cool. Repeat process with the remaining potato slices. You will not need to keep oiling the plate.

Nutrition Facts

Per Serving:

80.2 calories; protein 1.2g 2% DV; carbohydrates 11.6g 4% DV; fat 3.5g 5% DV; cholesterolmg; sodium 294.5mg 12% DV.

Microwave Baked Potato

Prep: 1 min **Cook:** 11 mins **Total:** 12 mins **Servings:** 1 **Yield:** 1 serving

Ingredients

- 1 large russet potato
- 1 tablespoon butter or margarine
- 3 tablespoons shredded Cheddar cheese
- 1 pinch salt and pepper to taste
- 3 teaspoons sour cream

Directions

- **Step 1**
  Scrub the potato, and prick several time with the tines of a fork. Place on a plate.
- **Step 2**
  Cook on full power in the microwave for 5 minutes. Turn over, and continue to cook for 5 more minutes. When the potato is soft, remove from the microwave, and cut in half lengthwise. Season with salt and pepper, and mash up the inside a little using a fork. Top the open sides with butter and 2 tablespoons of cheese. Return to the microwave, and cook for about 1 minute to melt the cheese.
- **Step 3**
  Top with remaining cheese and sour cream, and serve.

Nutrition Facts

Per Serving:

517.3 calories; protein 14.2g 29% DV; carbohydrates 65.4g 21% DV; fat 23.1g 36% DV; cholesterol 63.1mg 21% DV; sodium 421.6mg 17% DV.

Southwest Chicken Casserole

Servings: 4 **Yield:** 4 servings

Ingredients

- 1 (5 ounce) can chicken chunks, drained
- 1 (4 ounce) can diced green chiles
- 1 (10.75 ounce) can condensed cream of mushroom soup
- 2 cups shredded Cheddar cheese
- 2 tablespoons dried minced onion
- salt and pepper to taste
- 1 ¼ cups water
- 2 cups instant rice

Directions

- **Step 1**
  In a large bowl, combine the chicken, chiles, soup, cheese, onions, salt, pepper and water and pour the mixture into a microwave safe 9x13 inch casserole dish.
- **Step 2**
  Add the rice. The mixture should be the consistency of soupy pancake batter.
- **Step 3**
  Cover the dish with a lid or plastic wrap and microwave for about 15 minutes (depending on the microwave). Serve with mexicorn and green salad if desired.

Nutrition Facts

Per Serving:

543.6 calories; protein 27.1g 54% DV; carbohydrates 47.8g 15% DV; fat 26.5g 41% DV; cholesterol 81.3mg 27% DV; sodium 1354.8mg 54% DV.

Microwave Oven Peanut Brittle

Prep: 10 mins **Cook:** 20 mins **Total:** 30 mins **Servings:** 16 **Yield:** 1 pound

Ingredients

- 1 ½ cups dry roasted peanuts
- 1 cup white sugar
- ½ cup light corn syrup
- 1 pinch salt
- 1 tablespoon butter
- 1 teaspoon vanilla extract
- 1 teaspoon baking soda

Directions

- **Step 1**
  Grease a baking sheet, and set aside. In a glass bowl, combine peanuts, sugar, corn syrup, and salt. Cook in microwave for 6 to 7 minutes on High (700 W); mixture should be bubbly and peanuts browned. Stir in butter and vanilla; cook 2 to 3 minutes longer.
- **Step 2**
  Quickly stir in baking soda, just until mixture is foamy. Pour immediately onto greased baking sheet. Let cool 15 minutes, or until set. Break into pieces, and store in an airtight container.

Nutrition Facts

Per Serving:

164.6 calories; protein 3.2g 7% DV; carbohydrates 23.3g 8% DV; fat 7.5g 12% DV; cholesterol 1.9mg 1% DV; sodium 91mg 4% DV.

Shelby's Microwave Meat Loaf

Prep:20 mins**Cook:**15 mins**Additional:**10 mins **Total:** 45 mins **Servings:** 6 **Yield:** 6 servings

Ingredients

- 1 (8 ounce) can tomato sauce
- ¼ cup brown sugar
- 1 teaspoon prepared mustard
- 2 large eggs eggs, lightly beaten
- 1 onion, minced
- ¼ cup minced green bell pepper
- ¼ teaspoon garlic powder
- ½ cup saltine cracker crumbs
- 1 teaspoon salt
- ¼ teaspoon ground black pepper
- 2 pounds extra lean ground beef

Directions

- **Step 1**
  In a small bowl, mix together the tomato sauce, brown sugar, and mustard; stir until the brown sugar has dissolved.
- **Step 2**
  In a large mixing bowl, mix the eggs, minced onion and green pepper, garlic powder, cracker crumbs, salt, and black pepper; mix in the ground beef and half the tomato sauce mixture, stirring until the meat loaf is thoroughly combined. Place the meat mixture into a 2-quart microwave-safe baking dish. Spread the remaining tomato sauce mixture over the meat loaf.
- **Step 3**
  Cook in microwave oven on High setting until set, the juices run clear, and meat is no longer pink inside, 10 to 15 minutes depending on power of microwave oven. An instant-read meat thermometer, inserted into the center of the loaf, should read 165 degrees F (75 degrees C). Drain any grease from the dish as soon as loaf is cooked; allow to stand, uncovered, 10 to 15 minutes before serving.

Nutrition Facts

Per Serving:

382.1 calories; protein 29.5g 59% DV; carbohydrates 22.8g 7% DV; fat 18.8g 29% DV; cholesterol 147.6mg 49% DV; sodium 664.7mg 27% DV.

Schweineruckbraten (Microwave Loin of Pork)

Prep: 10 mins **Cook:** 22 mins **Total:** 32 mins **Servings:** 3 **Yield:** 3 servings

Ingredients

- 1 (2 pound) boneless pork loin
- 2 tablespoons chopped fresh rosemary
- ½ cup water
- 3 medium (2-1/2" dia)s onions, halved
- 1 teaspoon salt
- 1 teaspoon ground black pepper
- 1 teaspoon dried thyme
- 1 teaspoon ground cumin

Directions

- **Step 1**
  Pat the pork roast dry with a paper towel and perforate the meat at 1 inch intervals with a knife or fork. Insert leaves of rosemary in the perforations.
- **Step 2**
  Place the onion halves into a glass 9 or 10 inch pie plate. Set the meat on top of the onions so they act as a roasting rack. Pour the water over the meat and season with salt, pepper, thyme, and cumin.
- **Step 3**
  Cook in the microwave at full power for 16 minutes (or about 8 minutes per pound). Turn the roast over and cook for an additional 6 minutes or until the internal temperature of the roast has reached 145 degrees F (63 degrees C). Let the roast rest for about 15 minutes before carving and serving.

Nutrition Facts

Per Serving:

496 calories; protein 50.1g 100% DV; carbohydrates 11.6g 4% DV; fat 26.7g 41% DV; cholesterol 147.1mg 49% DV; sodium 888.6mg 36% DV.

Basic Microwave Risotto

Servings: 4 **Yield:** 4 servings

Ingredients

- 3 tablespoons butter
- 1 clove garlic, minced
- 1 onion, chopped
- 1 ½ cups vegetable broth
- 1 cup uncooked Arborio rice
- ¾ cup white wine
- ¼ cup grated Parmesan cheese

Directions

Step 1

In a 3 quart, microwave safe casserole dish combine butter, garlic and onion. Place dish in microwave and cook on high for 3 minutes.

Step 2

Place vegetable broth in a microwave safe dish. Heat on microwave until the broth is hot but not boiling (approximately 2 minutes).

Step 3

Stir the rice and broth into the casserole dish with the onion, butter and garlic mixture. Cover the dish tightly and cook on high for 6 minutes.

Step 4

Stir wine into the rice. Cook on high for 10 minutes more. Most of the liquid should boil off. Stir the cheese into the rice and serve.

Nutrition Facts

Per Serving:

367.8 calories; protein 7.1g 14% DV; carbohydrates 51.8g 17% DV; fat 10.6g 16% DV; cholesterol 28.4mg 10% DV; sodium 333mg 13% DV.

Gourmet Microwave Popcorn

Prep: 5 mins **Cook:** 5 mins **Total:** 10 mins **Servings:** 2 **Yield:** 2 cups

Ingredients

- ¼ cup unpopped popcorn
- 1 pinch salt to taste
- 1 teaspoon olive oil, or more if needed

Directions

- **Step 1**

  Place popcorn in a brown paper bag. Tightly seal the bag by folding the top several times.
- **Step 2**

  Microwave on High until the popping slows, about 2 minutes. Carefully open the bag. Season with salt and drizzle with olive oil. Reclose the bag and shake to distribute the seasoning.

Nutrition Facts

Per Serving:

113.8 calories; protein 3g 6% DV; carbohydrates 18.5g 6% DV; fat 3.6g 6% DV; cholesterolmg; sodium 0.8mg.

Microwave Corn on the Cob

Cook: 5 mins **Total:** 5 mins **Servings:** 1 **Yield:** 1 serving

Ingredients

- 1 ear corn, husked and cleaned

Directions

- **Step 1**
- Wet a paper towel, and wring out. Wrap the ear of corn in the moist towel, and place on a dinner plate. Cook in the microwave for 5 minutes. Carefully remove paper towel, and enjoy!

Nutrition Facts

Per Serving:

123 calories; protein 4.6g 9% DV; carbohydrates 27.2g 9% DV; fat 1.7g 3% DV; cholesterolmg; sodium 21.5mg 1% DV.

Microwave Chocolate Mug Cake

Prep: 5 mins **Cook:** 2 mins **Total:** 7 mins **Servings:** 1 **Yield:** 1 cake

Ingredients

- ¼ cup all-purpose flour
- ¼ cup white sugar
- 2 tablespoons unsweetened cocoa powder
- ⅛ teaspoon baking soda
- ⅛ teaspoon salt
- 3 tablespoons milk
- 2 tablespoons canola oil
- 1 tablespoon water
- ¼ teaspoon vanilla extract

Directions

- **Step 1**
  Mix flour, sugar, cocoa powder, baking soda, and salt in a large microwave-safe mug; stir in milk, canola oil, water, and vanilla extract.
- **Step 2**
  Cook in microwave until cake is done in the middle, about 1 minute 45 seconds.

Cook's Notes:

For a healthier version, use 1 1/2 tablespoons of plain unsweetened applesauce and use 3 tablespoons plus 1 teaspoon water instead of the milk.

Nutrition Facts

Per Serving:

603.1 calories; protein 6.9g 14% DV; carbohydrates 82g 26% DV; fat 30.4g 47% DV; cholesterol 3.7mg 1% DV; sodium 470.2mg 19% DV.

White Cranberry Walnut Nutmeg Fudge

Prep: 10 mins **Cook:** 4 mins **Additional:** 8 hrs **Total:** 8 hrs 14 mins **Servings:** 24 **Yield:** 1 9-inch square pan

Ingredients

- 1 teaspoon butter
- 3 cups white chocolate chips
- 1 (14 ounce) can sweetened condensed milk
- ⅓ cup butter
- 2 teaspoons rum flavoring
- 1 teaspoon vanilla extract
- ¼ teaspoon ground nutmeg, or to taste
- 1 cup sweetened dried cranberries (such as Craisins)
- 1 cup walnut pieces

Directions

- **Step 1**
  Grease a 9-inch square pan with 1 teaspoon butter.
- **Step 2**
  Combine white chocolate chips, sweetened condensed milk, and 1/3 cup butter in a microwave-safe bowl. Heat in the microwave until white chocolate starts to melt, about 3 minutes. Stir until smooth. Continue to microwave in 30-second intervals, stirring after each interval, until chocolate is completely melted.
- **Step 3**
  Stir rum flavoring, vanilla extract, and nutmeg into the white chocolate mixture. Fold in cranberries and walnut pieces. Pour fudge into the buttered baking pan, spreading it evenly into the corners.
- **Step 4**
  Let fudge cool until set, 8 hours to overnight.

Cook's Notes:

Try using dried apricot pieces or other dried fruit instead of the cranberries. If using dried apples, try using apple pie spice or ground cinnamon in place of some or all of the nutmeg.
Nutmeg varies a lot. You usually need less if you're grating it fresh than if you're using a five-year-old jar of ground nutmeg.

Nutrition Facts

Per Serving:

254 calories; protein 3.7g 7% DV; carbohydrates 26.5g 9% DV; fat 15.3g 24% DV; cholesterol 17.5mg 6% DV; sodium 64mg 3% DV.

Microwave Lemon Curd

Prep: 10 mins **Cook:** 6 mins **Total:** 16 mins **Servings:** 16 **Yield:** 2 cups

Ingredients

- 1 cup white sugar
- 3 large eggs eggs
- 1 cup fresh lemon juice
- 3 lemon (2-1/8" dia)s lemons, zested
- ½ cup unsalted butter, melted

Directions

- **Step 1**
  In a microwave-safe bowl, whisk together the sugar and eggs until smooth. Stir in lemon juice, lemon zest and butter. Cook in the microwave for one minute intervals, stirring after each minute until the mixture is thick enough to coat the back of a metal spoon. Remove from the microwave, and pour into small sterile jars. Store for up to three weeks in the refrigerator.

Tip

If you over cook the mixture a little, or forget to stir, you can pass the mixture through a fine sieve to remove the bits of cooked egg.

Nutrition Facts

Per Serving:

117 calories; protein 1.3g 3% DV; carbohydrates 14.1g 5% DV; fat 6.7g 10% DV; cholesterol 50.1mg 17% DV; sodium 14.1mg 1% DV.

Microwave Peanut Butter Chocolate Swirl Fudge

Prep: 10 mins **Cook:** 5 mins **Additional:** 1 hr **Total:** 1 hr 15 mins **Servings:** 60 **Yield:** 60 servings

Ingredients

- 1 (24 ounce) package white almond bark, broken in half
- 12 ounces peanut butter, or more to taste
- 3 (1.5 ounce) bars milk chocolate candy bars (such as Hershey's)

Directions

- **Step 1**
  Line an 8-inch square pan with waxed paper or spray with cooking spray.
- **Step 2**
  Place 1 almond bark half in a microwave-safe bowl; heat in the microwave, in 30-second intervals, stirring after each melting until smooth, 1 to 3 minutes. Add peanut butter to melted almond bark and mix well. Add the remaining almond bark to the bowl and push to the bottom of the bowl.
- **Step 3**

Heat mixture in the microwave for 1 minute; stir to break up any large pieces. Continue heating in microwave, in 30 second intervals, until completely melted. Pour fudge mixture into the prepared square pan.

- **Step 4**
  Melt chocolate bars in a microwave-safe bowl in 30-second intervals, stirring after each melting, for 1 to 3 minutes. Drizzle melted chocolate over fudge. Swirl the chocolate into the fudge using a knife.
- **Step 5**
  Refrigerate fudge until solid, about 1 hour.

Cook's Note:

If the mixture is refrigerated too long, it is hard to cut and breaks easily. It will soften some if left out at room temperature.

Nutrition Facts

Per Serving:

105.3 calories; protein 2.2g 4% DV; carbohydrates 9.1g 3% DV; fat 7.1g 11% DV; cholesterol 2.9mg 1% DV; sodium 37.2mg 2% DV.

Mom's Goulash in the Microwave

Prep: 10 mins **Cook:** 25 mins **Total:** 35 mins **Servings:** 6 **Yield:** 6 servings

Ingredients

- 1 (8 ounce) package uncooked elbow macaroni
- 1 pound ground beef
- 1 cup diced onion
- 1 cup sliced celery
- 1 tablespoon minced garlic
- 1 (14.5 ounce) can diced tomatoes
- 1 (10 ounce) can tomato sauce
- 1 tablespoon sugar
- 1 tablespoon paprika
- 1 teaspoon dried oregano
- ¼ teaspoon caraway seed
- 1 pinch cayenne pepper, or to taste
- 1 teaspoon salt

Directions

- **Step 1**
  Bring a pot of lightly salted water to a boil. Add the macaroni, and cook until tender, about 8 minutes. Drain.
- **Step 2**

Meanwhile, crumble the ground beef into a 2 quart or larger casserole dish. Add the onion, celery and garlic. Cook in the microwave on High for 5 to 6 minutes, or until beef is no longer pink. Stir once during cooking. Drain off the grease.

- **Step 3**
  Stir the tomatoes, tomato sauce and sugar into the beef, and season with paprika, oregano, caraway seed, cayenne pepper and salt. Cover, and cook in the microwave on power level 8 for about 14 minutes, or until celery is tender and the flavors have blended.
- **Step 4**
  Remove from the microwave, and mix in the cooked macaroni. Cook for 2 to 3 more minutes, until heated through. Serve.

Nutrition Facts

Per Serving:

326.7 calories; protein 19.4g 39% DV; carbohydrates 39.2g 13% DV; fat 9.8g 15% DV; cholesterol 45.9mg 15% DV; sodium 802.7mg 32% DV.

World's Best Bacon Cheese Dip

Prep: 15 mins **Cook:** 10 mins **Total:** 25 mins **Servings:** 16 **Yield:** 16 servings

Ingredients

- 4 slices bacon
- 1 (8 ounce) package cream cheese, softened
- 1 cup mayonnaise
- 8 ounces Swiss cheese, shredded
- 2 medium (4-1/8" long)s green onions, finely chopped
- 4 eaches buttery round crackers, crushed

Directions

- **Step 1**
  Place bacon in a large skillet. Cook over medium-high heat until evenly brown. Drain, crumble, and set aside.
- **Step 2**
  In a small bowl, mix the cream cheese with mayonnaise until smooth. Stir in Swiss cheese, onions, and bacon. Place bowl in microwave, and cook 2 minutes. Remove, and stir well. Return to microwave, and cook 2 to 4 minutes more. Sprinkle crushed crackers on top. Serve warm with crackers.

Nutrition Facts

Per Serving:

238.6 calories; protein 5.9g 12% DV; carbohydrates 2.3g 1% DV; fat 23.1g 36% DV; cholesterol 38.4mg 13% DV; sodium 213.4mg 9% DV.

Easy Microwave Chilaquiles

Prep: 15 mins **Cook:** 2 mins **Total:** 17 mins **Servings:** 4 **Yield:** 4 servings

Ingredients

- 1 ¾ cups enchilada sauce
- 1 (7-1/2 ounce) bag corn tortilla chips
- 2 cups sour cream
- 12 ounces shredded queso asadero (white Mexican cheese)

Directions

- **Step 1**
  Cover the bottom of a shallow microwaveable dish, with some of the enchilada sauce. Arrange a layer of tortilla chips on top. Follow with another layer of sauce, then a layer of sour cream. Sprinkle cheese over the top. Repeat layers to use up all ingredients, finishing with cheese on top.
- **Step 2**
  Cook in the microwave on high for 2 minutes, or until cheese has melted throughout. Serve immediately.

Nutrition Facts

Per Serving:

949.8 calories; protein 28.2g 56% DV; carbohydrates 46.6g 15% DV; fat 74.3g 114% DV; cholesterol 179.8mg 60% DV; sodium 858.1mg 34% DV.

Broccoli Cheese Soup VIII

Prep: 20 mins **Cook:** 20 mins **Total:** 40 mins **Servings:** 15 **Yield:** 15 cups

Ingredients

- 2 ½ (16 ounce) packages chopped frozen broccoli, thawed
- 2 cups half-and-half cream
- 4 cups water, divided
- 2 pounds processed cheese, cubed
- 1 teaspoon salt
- 1 teaspoon ground black pepper
- ½ teaspoon garlic powder

1 cup cornstarch**Directions**

- **Step 1**
  Steam the broccoli in a steamer or in a colander over boiling water until tender and bright green, 15 minutes. Set aside.
- **Step 2**

In a large microwave safe bowl, combine half-and-half, 2 cups water and cheese. Cook in microwave until cheese is melted and smooth, stirring every 2 minutes. Stir in salt, pepper and garlic powder and cook 2 minutes more. In a separate bowl, combine cornstarch and remaining 2 cups water, stirring to dissolve. Whisk the cornstarch mixture into the soup. Return the soup to the microwave, heating and stirring every 2 minutes until thick. Stir in broccoli; heat once more and serve.

Nutrition Facts

Per Serving:

294.6 calories; protein 14.3g 29% DV; carbohydrates 17.7g 6% DV; fat 19.2g 30% DV; cholesterol 60.4mg 20% DV; sodium 953mg 38% DV.

Jalapeno Popper Spread

Prep: 10 mins **Cook:** 3 mins **Total:** 13 mins **Servings:** 32 **Yield:** 4 cups

Ingredients

- 2 (8 ounce) packages cream cheese, softened
- 1 cup mayonnaise
- 1 (4 ounce) can chopped green chilies, drained
- 2 ounces canned diced jalapeno peppers, drained
- 1 cup grated Parmesan cheese

Directions

Step 1

Stir together cream cheese and mayonnaise in a large bowl until smooth. Stir in green chiles and jalapeno peppers. Pour mixture into a microwave safe serving dish, and sprinkle with Parmesan cheese.

Step 2

Microwave on High until hot, about 3 minutes.

Baked Variation

If you would like to brown the cheese, bake at 375 degrees F (190 degrees C) for about 30 minutes.

Nutrition Facts

Per Serving:

110.2 calories; protein 2.1g 4% DV; carbohydrates 1g; fat 11.1g 17% DV; cholesterol 20.2mg 7% DV; sodium 189mg 8% DV.

Sesame Udon Noodles

Prep: 20 mins **Cook:** 3 mins **Total:** 23 mins **Servings:** 4 **Yield:** 4 servings

Ingredients

- 2 cloves garlic, minced

- 1 tablespoon minced fresh ginger root
- ¼ cup soy sauce
- 3 tablespoons rice vinegar
- ¼ cup peanut oil
- 3 tablespoons sesame oil
- 1 dash hot pepper sauce
- ½ green bell pepper, julienned
- ½ red bell pepper, julienned
- ½ yellow bell pepper, julienned
- 4 medium (4-1/8" long)s green onions, minced
- 2 cups diagonally sliced snap peas
- 2 tablespoons sesame seeds, toasted
- 1 (7 ounce) package fresh udon noodles

Directions

- **Step 1**
  In a jar with a tight fitting lid, combine the garlic, ginger, soy sauce, rice vinegar, peanut oil, sesame oil and hot pepper sauce. Close the lid, and shake vigorously to blend. Set aside to let the flavors blend.
- **Step 2**
  Bring a large pot of water to a boil. Add udon noodles, and cook until tender, about 3 minutes. Drain, and place in a serving bowl.
- **Step 3**
  In a microwave-safe bowl, combine the green, red, and yellow peppers with green onion and peas. Heat in the microwave until warm, but still crisp. Add to the noodles in the bowl, and pour the dressing over all. Toss to coat everything in dressing, then sprinkle toasted sesame seeds over the top.

Toasting sesame seeds

Toast sesame seeds in a dry skillet over medium heat. Shake pan, or stir occasionally until lightly browned, about 3 minutes.

Nutrition Facts

Per Serving:

459.5 calories; protein 9.9g 20% DV; carbohydrates 45.1g 15% DV; fat 27g 42% DV; cholesterolmg; sodium 1205.8mg 48% DV.

Cheesy Chicken and Rice Casserole

Prep: 15 mins **Cook:** 30 mins **Total:** 45 mins **Servings:** 5 **Yield:** 4 to 6 servings

Ingredients

- 4 breast half, bone and skin removed (blank)s skinless, boneless chicken breast halves - cut into bite size pieces
- salt and pepper to taste
- 2 cups cooked white rice
- 1 (10.75 ounce) can condensed cream of chicken soup
- 2 cups shredded Cheddar cheese
- 3 slices soft white bread, cubed

Directions

- **Step 1**
  Preheat oven to 350 degrees F (175 degrees C).
- **Step 2**
  To Cook Chicken: Season chicken with salt and pepper to taste, place in a microwave-safe dish, cover and cook in microwave for 5 to 6 minutes. Turn and cook another 2 to 3 minutes or until cooked through and no longer pink inside. Let cool.
- **Step 3**
  In a 9x13 inch baking dish, combine chicken, rice and soup and mix well. Top with cheese, then with bread cubes.
- **Step 4**
  Bake at 350 degrees F (175 degrees C) for 20 minutes, or until cheese is melted and bubbly and bread is crunchy.

Nutrition Facts

Per Serving:

463 calories; protein 37.3g 75% DV; carbohydrates 30.3g 10% DV; fat 20.3g 31% DV; cholesterol 107.1mg 36% DV; sodium 844.4mg 34% DV.

Cinnamon Sugar Tortilla Delight

Prep: 2 mins **Cook:** 1 min **Total:** 3 mins **Servings:** 1 **Yield:** 1 tortilla

Ingredients

- 1 (10 inch) flour tortilla
- 2 teaspoons butter-flavored spread
- 1 ½ tablespoons cinnamon sugar

Directions

- **Step 1**
  Spread tortilla with butter-flavored spread; sprinkle with cinnamon sugar. Roll into a tube shape, then place on a microwave safe plate. Microwave on High for 30 seconds to warm.

Nutrition Facts

Per Serving:

361.4 calories; protein 5.8g 12% DV; carbohydrates 54.5g 18% DV; fat 13.5g 21% DV; cholesterol 1.2mg; sodium 508.7mg 20% DV.

Microwave English Muffin Bread

Prep: 10 mins **Cook:** 40 mins **Total:** 50 mins **Servings:** 12 **Yield:** 1 - 9x5 inch loaf

Ingredients

- 1 tablespoon yellow cornmeal
- ¼ cup warm water (110 degrees F/45 degrees C)
- 1 (.25 ounce) package active dry yeast
- 1 cup lukewarm milk
- 2 teaspoons white sugar
- 1 teaspoon salt
- ⅛ teaspoon baking soda
- 1 cup whole wheat flour
- 2 cups all-purpose flour

Directions

- **Step 1**
  Lightly grease a microwave-safe 9x5 inch loaf pan; sprinkle pan with cornmeal.
- **Step 2**
  In a large bowl, dissolve yeast in water. Add milk, sugar, salt, soda and whole wheat flour; beat well. Beat in all-purpose flour, 1/2 cup at a time, until a soft dough is formed. Turn dough out onto a lightly floured surface, and knead for about 5 minutes, or until smooth. Form into a loaf, and place into the prepared pan.
- **Step 3**
  Place in microwave oven uncovered, at 50 percent power, for 1 minute. Let rest for 10 minutes. Repeat 1 or 2 times until loaf has doubled in size.
- **Step 4**
  Microwave on high for 4 to 6 minutes, until top is no longer moist. Let stand for 5 minutes in pan. Remove and cool on a rack.

Nutrition Facts

Per Serving:

127 calories; protein 4.5g 9% DV; carbohydrates 25.6g 8% DV; fat 0.8g 1% DV; cholesterol 1.6mg 1% DV; sodium 216.5mg 9% DV.

Lemon Cake in a Mug

Prep: 10 mins **Cook:** 3 mins **Total:** 13 mins **Servings:** 1 **Yield:** 1 cake

Ingredients

Cake:

- 6 tablespoons all-purpose flour
- ¼ cup white sugar
- ⅛ teaspoon baking powder
- 1 egg
- 3 tablespoons vegetable oil
- 2 tablespoons water
- 1 tablespoon lemon juice

Sauce:

- 3 tablespoons white sugar
- 1 tablespoon lemon juice

Directions

- **Step 1**
  Combine flour, 1/4 cup white sugar, and baking powder together in a mug. Add egg, vegetable oil, water, and 1 tablespoon lemon juice; stir until well mixed.
- **Step 2**
  Cook in the microwave on high until cake is cooked through, 2 1/2 to 3 minutes. Remove from microwave and cool.
- **Step 3**
  Mix 3 tablespoons white sugar and 1 tablespoon lemon juice together in a microwave-safe bowl until smooth; cook in microwave until sauce is bubbling, about 30 seconds. Pour sauce over cake.

Nutrition Facts

Per Serving:

949.9 calories; protein 11.2g 23% DV; carbohydrates 126.4g 41% DV; fat 46.3g 71% DV; cholesterol 186mg 62% DV; sodium 133.1mg 5% DV.

Microwave Raisin Bread Pudding

Prep: 5 mins **Cook:** 25 mins **Total:** 30 mins **Servings:** 6 **Yield:** 1 - 2 quart pudding

Ingredients

- 16 thick slices raisin bread, cubed
- ½ cup white sugar
- ⅛ teaspoon ground cinnamon
- 2 cups milk

- ¼ cup butter
- 5 large eggs eggs, beaten
- ½ cup white sugar
- 1 teaspoon vanilla extract

Directions

- **Step 1**
  Line a microwave-safe 2 quart ring mold or baking dish with raisin bread. Sprinkle sugar and cinnamon evenly over bread cubes. Set aside.
- **Step 2**
  Place milk and butter in a 1 quart glass measure and microwave on medium 4 1/2 to 5 1/2 minutes, until butter is melted and milk is scalded. Quickly stir eggs, 1/2 cup sugar and vanilla into hot milk mixture. Pour over bread cubes.
- **Step 3**
  Cover with plastic wrap and microwave at medium heat for 17 to 19 minutes, until pudding is set.

Nutrition Facts

Per Serving:

533.1 calories; protein 14.7g 30% DV; carbohydrates 82.2g 27% DV; fat 17.2g 26% DV; cholesterol 181.8mg 61% DV; sodium 479mg 19% DV.

Cindy's Microwave Chicken Parmesan

Prep: 15 mins **Cook:** 18 mins **Additional:** 10 mins **Total:** 43 mins **Servings:** 4 **Yield:** 4 servings

Ingredients

- 4 eaches skinless, boneless chicken breasts
- 1 cup Italian-seasoned bread crumbs
- 1 cup grated Parmesan cheese
- 1 tablespoon smoked paprika
- 1 teaspoon dried parsley flakes
- 2 large eggs eggs
- 1 serving olive oil cooking spray
- 1 (28 ounce) jar chunky marinara sauce (such as Barilla)
- 2 cups shredded mozzarella cheese
- 2 teaspoons crushed oregano

Directions

- **Step 1**
  Place chicken breasts between 2 sheets of heavy plastic on a solid, level surface. Firmly pound with the smooth side of a meat mallet to 1/2-inch thickness.
- **Step 2**

Shake bread crumbs, Parmesan cheese, paprika, and parsley flakes together in a large resealable plastic bag.

- **Step 3**
  Beat eggs in a shallow bowl. Dip chicken breasts in beaten eggs; dredge in bread crumb mixture. Dip and dredge each chicken breast once more.
- **Step 4**
  Spray a microwave-safe dish large enough to hold chicken breasts in a single layer with cooking spray. Arrange breaded chicken breasts in the dish. Spray tops of the chicken breasts with cooking spray.
- **Step 5**
  Cook in the microwave at 50% power for 6 minutes. Pour marinara sauce over chicken breasts. Cover and cook at 100% power for 12 minutes. Sprinkle mozzarella cheese and oregano over sauce. Cover dish and let stand until mozzarella cheese melts, about 10 minutes.

Nutrition Facts

Per Serving:

668.9 calories; protein 54.4g 109% DV; carbohydrates 51g 17% DV; fat 26.6g 41% DV; cholesterol 209.2mg 70% DV; sodium 1973.2mg 79% DV.

Butternut Soup

Prep: 15 mins **Cook:** 35 mins **Total:** 50 mins **Servings:** 6 **Yield:** 6 servings

Ingredients

- 2 pounds butternut squash, cubed
- 2 medium (2-1/2" dia)s onions, chopped
- 1 tablespoon butter
- 4 cups vegetable broth
- ½ cup heavy cream
- salt and pepper to taste
- 1 dash ground nutmeg
- 1 dash ground cloves
- 1 dash ground cinnamon

Directions

- **Step 1**
  In a large microwave safe dish combine squash, onions and butter. Cover and microwave on high for 4 minutes. Peel squash. Stir in broth and cook on high for another 20 to 25 minutes, or until squash is tender. Puree squash, onions and broth in a food processor or blender. Add cream, salt and pepper, and microwave on high for another 3 to 4 minutes, or until heated through. Flavor with nutmeg, cloves and cinnamon to taste.

Nutrition Facts

Per Serving:

212 calories; protein 3.6g 7% DV; carbohydrates 31.2g 10% DV; fat 10g 15% DV; cholesterol 32.3mg 11% DV; sodium 338.5mg 14% DV.

Banana Nut Oatmeal

Prep: 5 mins **Cook:** 2 mins **Total:** 7 mins **Servings:** 1 **Yield:** 1 bowl of oatmeal

Ingredients

- ¼ cup quick cooking oats
- ½ cup skim milk
- 1 teaspoon flax seeds
- 2 tablespoons chopped walnuts
- 3 tablespoons honey
- 1 banana, peeled

Directions

- **Step 1**
  Combine the oats, milk, flax seeds, walnuts, honey, and banana in a microwave-safe bowl. Cook in microwave on High for 2 minutes. Mash the banana with a fork and stir into the mixture. Serve hot.

Nutrition Facts

Per Serving:

532.2 calories; protein 11.2g 22% DV; carbohydrates 101.7g 33% DV; fat 13.1g 20% DV; cholesterol 2.5mg 1% DV; sodium 57.8mg 2% DV.

Scrambled Eggs in a Mug

Prep: 5 mins **Cook:** 2 mins **Total:** 7 mins **Servings:** 1 **Yield:** 1 serving

Ingredients

- 1 egg
- 1 tablespoon milk
- 1 pinch ground black pepper

Directions

- **Step 1**
  Crack egg into a microwave-safe mug; beat until even in color. Pour in milk and beat until light yellow in color.
- **Step 2**
  Heat in microwave until cooked through and fluffy, about 90 seconds. Sprinkle pepper over egg.

Nutrition Facts

Per Serving:

81.7 calories; protein 6.9g 14% DV; carbohydrates 1.7g 1% DV; fat 5.3g 8% DV; cholesterol 187.2mg 62% DV; sodium 76.7mg 3% DV.

Easy Glazed Carrots

Prep: 5 mins **Cook:** 5 mins **Total:** 10 mins **Servings:** 4 **Yield:** 4 servings

Ingredients

- 1 (16 ounce) can sliced carrots, drained
- ⅔ cup brown sugar
- ¼ cup butter
- 2 tablespoons orange marmalade

Directions

- **Step 1**

  Place carrots into a microwave-safe bowl; add brown sugar, butter, and orange marmalade to carrots. Cover bowl loosely with plastic wrap and cook in microwave on high power for 3 minutes; stir. If butter and marmalade aren't completely melted, continue cooking on high power for 30-second intervals, stirring after each interval, until carrots are coated with glaze.

Nutrition Facts

Per Serving:

243.9 calories; protein 0.8g 2% DV; carbohydrates 36.4g 12% DV; fat 11.7g 18% DV; cholesterol 30.5mg 10% DV; sodium 362.9mg 15% DV.

Freeze-and-Reheat Breakfast Burritos

Prep: 30 mins **Cook:** 24 mins **Total:** 54 mins **Servings:** 10 **Yield:** 10 burritos

Ingredients

- 1 (12 ounce) package bacon
- 10 large eggs
- 3 tablespoons milk
- ¼ teaspoon salt
- 3 tablespoons vegetable oil
- 4 cups frozen hash brown potatoes with peppers and onion (such as Ore-Ida Potatoes O'Brien)
- ½ teaspoon garlic salt
- ¼ teaspoon ground black pepper
- 10 large flour tortillas
- 1 ½ cups shredded Cheddar cheese
- 1 cup salsa, or to taste

Directions

- **Step 1**
  Place bacon in a large skillet and cook over medium-high heat, turning occasionally, until evenly browned, about 10 minutes. Drain on paper towels and crumble into bits. Keep skillet warm.
- **Step 2**
  Whisk eggs, milk, and salt together in a bowl. Pour into the hot skillet. Cook and stir over medium-high heat until eggs are set, about 5 minutes. Transfer to a bowl.
- **Step 3**
  Heat oil in same skillet over medium-high heat. Add frozen potatoes, garlic salt, and pepper. Fry until browned on the bottom, 4 to 5 minutes. Flip and cook until other side is browned, 4 to 5 minutes more. Let cool.
- **Step 4**
  Cut 10 squares of aluminum foil slightly larger than the tortillas. Lay 1 tortilla on each square; evenly distribute Cheddar cheese on top. Add eggs, bacon, salsa, and potatoes to each tortilla, in that order. Tightly roll the burritos, tucking tops and bottoms in first.
- **Step 5**
  Wrap aluminum foil tightly around each burrito, covering it completely. Place in resealable plastic bags in a single layer. Remove as much air as possible from the bags before sealing. Store in the freezer until ready to reheat.
- **Step 6**
  Reheat by removing the aluminum foil, placing the burrito on a microwave-safe plate, and topping it with a paper towel. Heat in the microwave until evenly warmed through, 1 to 2 minutes.

Nutrition Facts

Per Serving:

545.7 calories; protein 23.1g 46% DV; carbohydrates 54.8g 18% DV; fat 29.5g 46% DV; cholesterol 216.5mg 72% DV; sodium 1268.6mg 51% DV.

Quick and Easy Grilled Potatoes

Prep: 5 mins **Cook:** 22 mins **Total:** 27 mins **Servings:** 4 **Yield:** 4 servings

Ingredients

- 2 large russet potatoes, scrubbed
- 2 tablespoons olive oil
- 1 pinch salt and ground black pepper to taste

Directions

- **Step 1**
  Poke each potato with the tines of a fork. Place the potatoes in a microwave oven, and cook on high power for about 5 minutes. Check about halfway through, and turn potatoes over for even cooking. Slice each potato in half the long way and cook potatoes another 2 minutes on high power.

- **Step 2**
  Preheat a grill for medium heat.
- **Step 3**
  Brush the potato tops with olive oil, and season with salt and pepper to taste.
- **Step 4**
  Cook on prepared grill for 15 to 20 minutes, turning once.

Nutrition Facts

Per Serving:

202.8 calories; protein 3.7g 8% DV; carbohydrates 32.2g 10% DV; fat 6.9g 11% DV; cholesterolmg; sodium 11.1mg.

Instant Chocolate Hard Shell

Prep: 5 mins **Cook:** 1 min **Total:** 6 mins **Servings:** 32 **Yield:** 2 cups

Ingredients

- 2 cups semisweet chocolate chips
- ⅔ cup coconut oil

Directions

- **Step 1**
- Combine chocolate chips and coconut oil in a microwave-safe bowl; heat in microwave in 30-second intervals, mixing well each time, until mixture is smooth, 1 to 2 minutes. It takes about 1 minute of stirring until they fully mix together. Store at room temperature in an air-tight container.

Cook's Note:

Add more oil for thinner, crispier hard shell and add less for a thicker hard shell.

Nutrition Facts

Per Serving:

89.4 calories; protein 0.4g 1% DV; carbohydrates 6.6g 2% DV; fat 7.7g 12% DV; cholesterolmg; sodium 1.2mg.

Corn on the Cob in the Microwave

Prep: 5 mins **Cook:** 8 mins **Total:** 13 mins **Servings:** 4 **Yield:** 4 servings

Ingredients

- 4 ears fresh corn, shucked
- 4 dampened paper towels
- 1 storage bag

Directions

- **Step 1**
  Wrap each ear of corn in a damp paper towel. Place corn in a storage bag; do not seal the bag.
- **Step 2**

Place in the microwave oven and cook on high for 4 minutes. Flip the bag over and cook on high an additional 4 minutes.

Nutrition Facts

Per Serving:

77.4 calories; protein 2.9g 6% DV; carbohydrates 17.1g 6% DV; fat 1.1g 2% DV; cholesterolmg; sodium 13.5mg 1% DV.

Microwave Nutella Mug Cake

Prep: 10 mins **Cook:** 3 mins **Total:** 13 mins **Servings:** 1 **Yield:** 1 very large mug of cake

Ingredients

- ¼ cup self-rising flour
- ¼ cup white sugar
- 1 egg, beaten
- 3 tablespoons cocoa powder
- 3 tablespoons chocolate-hazelnut spread (such as Nutella)
- 3 tablespoons milk
- 3 tablespoons vegetable oil

Directions

- **Step 1**

  Beat flour, sugar, egg, cocoa powder, chocolate-hazelnut spread, milk, and vegetable oil together in a large coffee mug with a fork until smooth.
- **Step 2**

  Cook in microwave oven on High until cooked in the center, 90 seconds to 3 minutes.

Cook's Note:

Due to variations in microwave oven wattage, times may vary.

Nutrition Facts

Per Serving:

1036.9 calories; protein 17.1g 34% DV; carbohydrates 113g 37% DV; fat 62.8g 97% DV; cholesterol 189.7mg 63% DV; sodium 534mg 21% DV.

Corn On The Cob (Easy Cleaning and Shucking)

Prep: 10 mins **Cook:** 5 mins **Total:** 15 mins **Servings:** 1 **Yield:** 1 serving

Ingredients

- 1 ear corn on the cob, unhusked
- 1 teaspoon butter, or to taste
- 1 pinch salt to taste

Directions

- **Step 1**
  Place ear of corn in a microwave oven and cook on high for 2 minutes; flip corn over and cook on high until kernels are hot and steaming, another 2 minutes.
- **Step 2**
  Place corn ear on a cutting board, using a pot holder or folded kitchen towel, and cut off the bottom of the ear, exposing 1/4 to 1/2 inch of kernels. Hold the ear from the top and squeeze ear of corn out of the husk from top to bottom. Husks and silk will be left behind.
- **Step 3**
  Spread ear with butter and season with salt.

Nutrition Facts

Per Serving:

113.3 calories; protein 2.9g 6% DV; carbohydrates 17.1g 6% DV; fat 5.1g 8% DV; cholesterol 10.8mg 4% DV; sodium 42.3mg 2% DV.

Simple French Toast in a Cup

Prep: 5 mins **Cook:** 5 mins **Total:** 10 mins **Servings:** 1 **Yield:** 1 serving

Ingredients

- 1 tablespoon butter
- ¼ cup milk
- 1 egg, beaten
- ¼ teaspoon ground cinnamon
- ¼ teaspoon white sugar
- ¼ teaspoon vanilla extract
- 2 slices bread, cut into cubes

Directions

- **Step 1**
  Melt butter in the bottom of a large microwave-safe mug in the microwave, about 30 seconds. Tilt mug to coat all sides with melted butter.
- **Step 2**
  Stir melted butter, milk, egg, cinnamon, sugar, and vanilla extract together in the mug. Press bread cubes into milk mixture.
- **Step 3**
  Microwave on High until set, about 90 seconds.

Nutrition Facts

Per Serving:

345.4 calories; protein 12.3g 25% DV; carbohydrates 30.2g 10% DV; fat 19.3g 30% DV; cholesterol 221.4mg 74% DV; sodium 517.5mg 21% DV.

Easy Mochi

Prep: 30 mins **Cook:** 5 mins **Additional:** 3 hrs **Total:** 3 hrs 35 mins **Servings:** 8 **Yield:** 8 servings

Ingredients

- 1 cup sweetened red bean paste
- 1 cup sweet rice flour (mochiko)
- 1 teaspoon green tea powder (matcha)
- 1 cup water
- ¼ cup white sugar
- ½ cup cornstarch, for rolling out the dough

Directions

- **Step 1**
  Wrap red bean paste in aluminum foil and place in the freezer for at least 3 hours. Mix sweet rice flour and green tea powder thoroughly in a microwave-safe glass or ceramic bowl. Stir in water, then sugar. Mix until smooth. Cover bowl with plastic wrap.
- **Step 2**
  Cook the rice flour mixture in the microwave for 3 minutes and 30 seconds. Meanwhile, remove red bean paste from the freezer and divide paste into 8 equal balls. Set aside. Stir rice flour mixture and heat for another 15 to 30 seconds.
- **Step 3**
  Dust work surface with cornstarch. While the mochi is still hot from the microwave, begin rolling balls the size of about 2 tablespoons. Flatten the mochi ball and place 1 frozen red bean paste ball in the center. Pinch the mochi over the red bean paste until the paste is completely covered. Sprinkle with additional cornstarch and place mochi seam side down in a paper muffin liner to prevent sticking. Repeat until all the mochi and red bean paste is used.

Nutrition Facts

Per Serving:

213.2 calories; protein 2.8g 6% DV; carbohydrates 49.8g 16% DV; fat 0.2g; cholesterolmg; sodium 82.3mg 3% DV.

No Egg Chocolate Mug Cake

Prep: 5 mins **Cook:** 2 mins **Total:** 7 mins **Servings:** 1 **Yield:** 1 mug cake

Ingredients

- 4 tablespoons all-purpose flour
- 4 tablespoons white sugar

- 3 tablespoons milk
- 2 tablespoons unsweetened cocoa powder
- ½ tablespoon olive oil
- 1 pinch baking powder
- 1 tablespoon semisweet chocolate chips
- 1 tablespoon sliced almonds

Directions

- **Step 1**

  Combine flour, sugar, milk, cocoa powder, olive oil, and baking powder in a large mug and mix well. Stir in chocolate chips and almonds.
- **Step 2**

  Place mug in the microwave and cook until cake has risen by 50 percent, 30 seconds to 2 minutes.

Nutrition Facts

Per Serving:

586.3 calories; protein 9.3g 19% DV; carbohydrates 101.1g 33% DV; fat 20.9g 32% DV; cholesterol 3.7mg 1% DV; sodium 130.9mg 5% DV.

90-Second Keto Bread in a Mug

Prep: 5 mins **Cook:** 2 mins **Additional:** 2 mins **Total:** 9 mins **Servings:** 1 **Yield:** 1 serving

Ingredients

- 1 tablespoon butter
- ⅓ cup blanched almond flour
- 1 egg
- ½ teaspoon baking powder
- 1 pinch salt

Directions

- **Step 1**

  Place butter in a microwave-safe mug. Microwave until melted, about 15 seconds. Swirl mug until fully coated.
- **Step 2**

  Combine almond flour, egg, baking powder, and salt in the mug; whisk until smooth.
- **Step 3**

  Microwave at maximum power until set, about 90 seconds. Let cool for 2 minutes before slicing.

Nutrition Facts

Per Serving:

408 calories; protein 14.5g 29% DV; carbohydrates 9.8g 3% DV; fat 36.4g 56% DV; cholesterol 194.2mg 65% DV; sodium 542.2mg 22% DV.

Fluffy Microwave Scrambled Eggs

Prep: 5 mins **Cook:** 5 mins **Total:** 10 mins **Servings:** 2 **Yield:** 2 servings

Ingredients

- 4 eaches eggs
- ¼ cup milk
- ⅛ teaspoon salt

Directions

- **Step 1**
  Break the eggs into a microwave-proof mixing bowl. Add milk and salt; mix well.
- **Step 2**
  Pop the bowl into the microwave and cook on high power for 30 seconds. Remove bowl, beat eggs very well, scraping down the sides of the bowl, and return to the microwave for another 30 seconds. Repeat this pattern, stirring every 30 seconds for up to 2 1/2 minutes. Stop when eggs have the consistency you desire.

Nutrition Facts

Per Serving:

141.1 calories; protein 12.1g 24% DV; carbohydrates 2.1g 1% DV; fat 9.3g 14% DV; cholesterol 329.8mg 110% DV; sodium 281mg 11% DV.

Microwave Popcorn

Prep: 2 mins **Cook:** 3 mins **Total:** 5 mins **Servings:** 3 **Yield:** 3 servings

Ingredients

- ½ cup unpopped popcorn
- 1 teaspoon vegetable oil
- ½ teaspoon salt, or to taste

Directions

- **Step 1**
  In a cup or small bowl, mix together the unpopped popcorn and oil. Pour the coated corn into a brown paper lunch sack, and sprinkle in the salt. Fold the top of the bag over twice to seal in the ingredients.
- **Step 2**
  Cook in the microwave at full power for 2 1/2 to 3 minutes, or until you hear pauses of about 2 seconds between pops. Carefully open the bag to avoid steam, and pour into a serving bowl.

Note

A few kernels will remain unpopped. Longer cooking may pop the rest, but will burn some of the already-popped kernels, so it is not recommended.

Nutrition Facts

Per Serving:

137.1 calories; protein 4.1g 8% DV; carbohydrates 24.6g 8% DV; fat 3.1g 5% DV; cholesterolmg; sodium 388.6mg 16% DV.

Microwave Corn-on-the-Cob in the Husk

Prep: 5 mins **Cook:** 5 mins **Total:** 10 mins **Servings:** 1 **Yield:** 1 serving

Ingredients

- 1 ear fresh corn in the husk

Directions

- **Step 1**

  Rinse entire ear of corn under water briefly. Wrap corn in a paper towel and place on a microwave-safe plate.
- **Step 2**

  Cook corn in the microwave oven until hot and cooked through, 3 to 5 minutes. Remove from microwave and let rest for 2 minutes. Remove corn husk.

Cook's Note:

Cooking time is variable. I cook 1 large ear for 5 minutes in a 1000 watt oven. If you have small ears of corn you will need to adjust the time.

No need to remove the corn silk. When you take the husk off the silk comes right along with it and your corn is as clean as it can be. Because the corn is hot I use a clean dish cloth to hold and remove the husk.

Nutrition Facts

Per Serving:

77.4 calories; protein 2.9g 6% DV; carbohydrates 17.1g 6% DV; fat 1.1g 2% DV; cholesterolmg; sodium 13.5mg 1% DV.

Quick and Simple Broccoli and Cheese

Prep: 5 mins **Cook:** 15 mins **Total:** 20 mins **Servings:** 4 **Yield:** 4 servings

Ingredients

- 1 (10 ounce) package frozen broccoli florets, thawed
- 3 tablespoons butter, melted
- salt and pepper to taste
- ½ cup shredded Cheddar cheese

Directions

- **Step 1**

- Place broccoli in a steamer over 1 inch of boiling water, and cover. Cook until tender but still firm, about 2 to 6 minutes. Drain and transfer to a microwave safe casserole dish.

- **Step 2**
- Pour melted butter over broccoli (use more or less, to taste) and season with salt and pepper. Sprinkle cheese over the top and microwave, on high, for 1 minute, or until cheese is melted.

Nutrition Facts

Per Serving:

151.7 calories; protein 5.6g 11% DV; carbohydrates 3.6g 1% DV; fat 13.5g 21% DV; cholesterol 37.7mg 13% DV; sodium 166.1mg 7% DV.

Grilled Asian Chicken

Prep: 15 mins **Cook:** 15 mins **Additional:** 20 mins **Total:** 50 mins **Servings:** 4 **Yield:** 4 servings

Ingredients

- ¼ cup soy sauce
- 4 teaspoons sesame oil
- 2 tablespoons honey
- 3 slices fresh ginger root
- 2 cloves garlic, crushed
- 4 breast half, bone and skin removed (blank)s skinless, boneless chicken breast halves

Directions

- **Step 1**
  In a small microwave-safe bowl, combine the soy sauce, oil, honey, ginger root, and garlic. Heat in microwave on medium for 1 minute, then stir. Heat again for 30 seconds, watching closely to prevent boiling.
- **Step 2**
  Place chicken breasts in a shallow dish. Pour soy sauce mixture over, and set aside to marinate for 15 minutes.
- **Step 3**
  Preheat a grill for medium-high heat. Drain marinade from chicken into a small saucepan. Bring to a boil, and simmer over medium heat for 5 minutes. Set aside for basting.
- **Step 4**
  Lightly oil the grill grate. Cook chicken on the prepared grill 6 to 8 minutes per side, or until juices run clear. Baste frequently with remaining marinade. Chicken will turn a beautiful golden brown.

Note:

The nutrition data for this recipe includes information for the full amount of the marinade ingredients. Depending on marinating time, ingredients, cooking method, etc., the actual amount of the marinade consumed will vary.

Nutrition Facts

Per Serving:

216.6 calories; protein 25.7g 51% DV; carbohydrates 10.6g 3% DV; fat 7.6g 12% DV; cholesterol 67.2mg 22% DV; sodium 961.3mg 39% DV.

Easy Microwave Chocolate Cake

Prep: 6 mins **Cook:** 2 mins **Total:** 8 mins **Servings:** 2 **Yield:** 2 servings

Ingredients

- 3 tablespoons butter, softened
- ¼ cup white sugar
- 1 egg
- 1 teaspoon vanilla extract
- ¼ cup milk
- ½ cup all-purpose flour
- 2 tablespoons cocoa powder
- ¼ teaspoon baking powder
- 1 pinch salt

Directions

- **Step 1**
  Spray a medium microwave-safe bowl with non-stick spray and set aside. In a mixing bowl, combine the butter, sugar, egg, vanilla extract, and milk; blend together. Combine the flour, cocoa powder, baking powder and salt; blend into the mixture until smooth. Pour into greased bowl.
- **Step 2**
  Cover and cook in the microwave on high for 2 to 2 1/2 minutes, or until cake springs back when touched. Since all microwaves cook differently, adjust the cooking time to accommodate your machine. To serve, let the cake cool five minutes, then cover the bowl with a plate and turn both bowl and plate upside down so the cake falls onto the plate.

Nutrition Facts

Per Serving:

433.1 calories; protein 8.6g 17% DV; carbohydrates 53.8g 17% DV; fat 21.4g 33% DV; cholesterol 141.2mg 47% DV; sodium 233.1mg 9% DV.

Microwave Bread and Butter Pickles

Prep: 20 mins **Cook:** 10 mins **Total:** 30 mins **Servings:** 24 **Yield:** 3 cups

Ingredients

- 1 large cucumber, sliced
- 1 teaspoon salt
- 1 onion, thinly sliced
- ½ teaspoon mustard seeds
- 1 cup white sugar
- ½ cup distilled white vinegar
- ¼ teaspoon celery seed
- ¼ teaspoon ground turmeric

Directions

- **Step 1**
  In a medium microwave safe bowl, mix cucumber, salt, onion, mustard seeds, white sugar, distilled white vinegar, celery seed and turmeric.
- **Step 2**
  Microwave on high 7 to 8 minutes, stirring twice, until cucumbers are tender and onion is translucent.
- **Step 3**
  Transfer to sterile containers. Seal and chill in the refrigerator until serving.

Nutrition Facts

Per Serving:

36.5 calories; protein 0.2g; carbohydrates 9.2g 3% DV; fatg; cholesterolmg; sodium 97.4mg 4% DV.

Microwave Mochi

Prep: 5 mins **Cook:** 10 mins **Total:** 15 mins **Servings:** 25 **Yield:** 25 servings

Ingredients

- 1 ½ cups mochiko (glutinous rice flour)
- 1 cup white sugar
- 1 ½ cups water
- 2 drops distilled white vinegar
- ½ cup potato starch
- ¼ cup white sugar
- ¼ teaspoon salt

Directions

- **Step 1**
  In a medium bowl, mix together the mochiko, 1 cup of sugar, and water until well blended. Mix in the 2 drops of vinegar to soften. Pour into a microwave-safe dish, and loosely cover with plastic. Microwave for 8 to 10 minutes on HIGH. Remove, and let cool until cool enough to handle.
- **Step 2**
  In a small bowl, combine the potato starch, 1/4 cup sugar, and salt. Turn the mochi out onto the plastic, and cut into pieces using a plastic or wooden knife. Metal knives tend to stick too much. Roll the pieces in the potato starch mixture.

Nutrition Facts

Per Serving:

82.5 calories; protein 0.6g 1% DV; carbohydrates 19.9g 6% DV; fat 0.1g; cholesterolmg; sodium 23.5mg 1% DV.

Loaded Potato Soup I

Prep: 15 mins **Cook:** 15 mins **Total:** 30 mins **Servings:** 12 **Yield:** 12 servings

Ingredients

- 8 medium (2-1/4" to 3" dia, raw)s potatoes, peeled and cubed
- ½ cup butter
- ½ cup all-purpose flour
- 8 cups milk
- ¼ cup chopped onion
- 1 (8 ounce) container sour cream
- ½ cup shredded Cheddar cheese
- 1 pinch salt and pepper to taste

Directions

- **Step 1**
  Place cubed potatoes into a glass dish, and cook in the microwave oven for 7 to 10 minutes, or until soft.
- **Step 2**
  While the potatoes are cooking, melt the butter in a large pot over medium-high heat. Whisk in flour until smooth, then gradually stir in the milk. Bring to a boil, then reduce heat to medium, and simmer for 5 to 10 minutes, or until slightly thickened.
- **Step 3**
  Stir in the potatoes and onion, and cook for 5 more minutes. Stir in the sour cream and Cheddar cheese until melted and well blended. Season with salt and pepper.

Nutrition Facts

Per Serving:

338.3 calories; protein 10.7g 21% DV; carbohydrates 37.6g 12% DV; fat 16.6g 26% DV; cholesterol 46.6mg 16% DV; sodium 169.2mg 7% DV.

PBM Sandwich

Prep: 4 mins **Cook:** 1 min **Total:** 5 mins **Servings:** 1 **Yield:** 1 sandwich

Ingredients

- 2 tablespoons peanut butter
- 2 slices bread
- 2 ½ tablespoons marshmallow cream (such as Marshmallow Fluff)

Directions

- **Step 1**
  Spread the peanut butter onto one slice of bread. Spread the marshmallow creme onto the other slice. Place the bread topping-side-up onto a microwave-safe plate. Cook in the microwave on High for 30 seconds. Place the two halves together and serve.

Nutrition Facts

Per Serving:

372.5 calories; protein 12.1g 24% DV; carbohydrates 43.5g 14% DV; fat 18.1g 28% DV; cholesterolmg; sodium 501.8mg 20% DV.

Homemade Pumpkin Puree in the Microwave

Prep: 15 mins **Cook:** 15 mins **Additional:** 10 mins **Total:** 40 mins **Servings:** 4 **Yield:** 4 cups

Ingredients

- 1 pie pumpkin

Directions

- **Step 1**
  Cut stem off of pumpkin to create a hole using a good, strong knife, as cutting through a pumpkin can be tricky. Scoop and scrape pulp and seeds out of pumpkin, saving seeds to roast later. Cut pumpkin in quarters. Cut quarters in 1/2 again.

- **Step 2**
  Place pumpkin pieces in a microwave-safe bowl. Cover tightly with plastic wrap, tight enough to not let any steam or moisture escape during cooking time.
- **Step 3**
  Microwave for 7 minutes, checking seal of plastic wrap halfway through cooking time to ensure no moisture is not escaping. Continue cooking in the microwave for another 8 minutes. Remove plastic wrap by pulling wrap furthest from you back towards you, allowing hot steam to escape away from you. Let cool for 10 minutes.

- **Step 4**
  Peel skin from pumpkin using your fingers.
- **Step 5**
  Puree peeled pumpkin using a food processor, hand masher, or a potato ricer.

Cook's Note:

Be sure the pieces are uniform in size to ensure even cooking.

Nutrition Facts

Per Serving:

88.4 calories; protein 3.4g 7% DV; carbohydrates 22.1g 7% DV; fat 0.3g 1% DV; cholesterolmg; sodium 3.4mg.

BBQ Chicken Chopped Salad

Prep: 20 mins **Cook:** 1 min **Total:** 21 mins **Servings:** 6 **Yield:** 6 servings

Ingredients

- 1 head romaine lettuce, chopped
- 1 (15 ounce) can black beans, rinsed and drained
- 1 (15 ounce) can sweet corn, drained
- 1 red bell pepper, chopped
- 1 cup peeled, shredded jicama
- 1 cup shredded carrots
- 4 eaches scallions, thinly sliced
- ¼ cup chopped fresh basil
- ¼ cup chopped fresh cilantro
- 3 fruit (2" dia)s limes, divided
- 1 (6 ounce) package cooked chicken breast strips (such as Foster Farms)
- 2 tablespoons barbeque sauce
- 1 avocado - peeled, pitted, and cubed

Directions

- **Step 1**
  Mix lettuce, black beans, corn, red bell pepper, jicama, carrots, scallions, basil, and cilantro together in a large bowl. Juice 2 limes and drizzle juice over salad; toss lightly.
- **Step 2**
  Combine chicken and barbeque sauce in a microwave-safe bowl; heat in microwave until chicken is warmed through, about 45 seconds.
- **Step 3**

Arrange chicken and avocado on top of the salad and squeeze remaining lime over salad.

Cook's Note:

I prefer the southwestern flavor for the chicken strips.

Drizzle extra BBQ sauce on top of salad if desired.

Nutrition Facts

Per Serving:

279.7 calories; protein 16.3g 33% DV; carbohydrates 40.6g 13% DV; fat 8.3g 13% DV; cholesterol 21.3mg 7% DV; sodium 580.8mg 23% DV.

Apple Crisp in a Mug

Prep: 10 mins **Cook:** 2 mins **Total:** 12 mins **Servings:** 1 **Yield:** 1 mug

Ingredients

- 1 tablespoon butter, softened
- 1 tablespoon white sugar
- 2 tablespoons all-purpose flour
- 2 tablespoons oats
- 4 dashes ground cinnamon, divided
- 1 pinch salt
- ½ apple - peeled, cored, and thinly sliced
- 1 tablespoon brown sugar
- 2 teaspoons water

Directions

- **Step 1**
  Combine butter and white sugar in a bowl using your fingers. Add flour, oats, 3 dashes cinnamon, and salt; mix until crumbly.
- **Step 2**
  Grease a mug; flatten 1/2 the crumble mixture into the bottom to form a crust.
- **Step 3**
  Microwave crust for 30 seconds on high.
- **Step 4**
  Remove mug from microwave; add 1 dash cinnamon, apple slices, and brown sugar. Add water. Mix apples, brown sugar, and cinnamon together carefully without disturbing crust. Pour remaining crumble mixture on top.
- **Step 5**
  Microwave for 1 minute and 50 seconds on 60% power. Remove from microwave; let cool about 1 minute.

Cook's Note:

If you like a tart apple crisp, then you can use less sugar. The amount you take out is up to you based on how sweet you like it. You may want to give the original recipe a try before messing with how much sugar you put in.

Nutrition Facts

Per Serving:

343.1 calories; protein 3.4g 7% DV; carbohydrates 57.4g 19% DV; fat 12.5g 19% DV; cholesterol 30.5mg 10% DV; sodium 242.6mg 10% DV.

Twice Microwaved Potatoes

Prep: 15 mins **Cook:** 30 mins **Total:** 45 mins **Servings:** 12 **Yield:** 12 servings

Ingredients

- 6 medium russet potatoes
- 4 medium (4-1/8" long)s green onions, chopped
- 1 cup sour cream
- ½ cup cubed processed cheese
- ¼ cup shredded Cheddar cheese
- 1 pinch garlic powder to taste
- 1 pinch seasoned salt to taste
- 1 pinch ground black pepper to taste
- 1 tablespoon chopped green onion
- ¼ cup shredded Cheddar cheese

Directions

- **Step 1**
  Poke potatoes with the tines of a fork, and place them in the microwave oven. The more holes, the better. Cook on high power for about 4 minutes per potato. Check about halfway through, and turn potatoes over for even cooking. Potatoes are done when they can be easily poked with a fork.
- **Step 2**
  Remove potatoes from the microwave, and cut each one in half lengthwise. Use a large spoon to scoop out the inside of the potatoes, leaving the skins intact. Place the scoopings into a large microwave safe bowl, and stir in the 4 green onions, sour cream, processed cheese, and 1/4 cup Cheddar cheese. Season with garlic powder, seasoned salt, and black pepper; mix well.
- **Step 3**
  Place the bowl in the microwave, and cook for 2 to 3 minutes, or until heated through. Scoop the mixture back into the potato skins to serve, or serve from the bowl. Garnish with additional green onion and shredded cheese if desired.

Nutrition Facts

Per Serving:

170 calories; protein 5.6g 11% DV; carbohydrates 20g 7% DV; fat 7.9g 12% DV; cholesterol 20.3mg 7% DV; sodium 167.4mg 7% DV.

Buttery Lemon Spinach

Prep: 5 mins **Cook:** 2 mins **Total:** 7 mins **Servings:** 6 **Yield:** 6 servings

Ingredients

- 2 (10 ounce) bags pre-washed fresh spinach
- 2 tablespoons garlic, minced
- 5 tablespoons butter
- 2 tablespoons lemon juice

Directions

- **Step 1**

  Rinse the spinach and place the leaves into a microwavable serving dish. Add the butter, garlic and lemon juice. Cover with plastic wrap. Steam in the microwave until the butter is melted and spinach is wilted, about 2 minutes. Remove the plastic wrap and toss to distribute seasoning before serving.

Nutrition Facts

Per Serving:

112 calories; protein 3g 6% DV; carbohydrates 4.8g 2% DV; fat 10g 15% DV; cholesterol 25.4mg 9% DV; sodium 143.5mg 6% DV.

Single-Serve Blueberry Crisp

Prep: 5 mins **Cook:** 5 mins **Total:** 10 mins **Servings:** 1 **Yield:** 1 serving

Ingredients

- ¾ cup fresh blueberries
- 2 teaspoons white sugar
- 1 teaspoon all-purpose flour
- ½ teaspoon vanilla extract
- 3 tablespoons rolled oats
- 1 tablespoon brown sugar
- 1 tablespoon all-purpose flour
- 2 teaspoons butter, melted

Directions

- **Step 1**

  Place blueberries, white sugar, 1 teaspoon flour, and vanilla extract in a microwave-safe bowl. Cook in a microwave oven for 30 seconds.

- **Step 2**

Mix together oats, brown sugar, 1 tablespoon flour, and butter in another microwave-safe bowl. Cook in a microwave oven for 30 seconds and combine with berry mixture.

Cook's Note:

You can use frozen blueberries instead of fresh. Microwave for 1 minute instead.

Nutrition Facts

Per Serving:

319.7 calories; protein 4g 8% DV; carbohydrates 56g 18% DV; fat 9.6g 15% DV; cholesterol 21.5mg 7% DV; sodium 63.8mg 3% DV.

Avocado and Black Bean Dip

Prep: 10 mins **Cook:** 1 min **Total:** 11 mins **Servings:** 4 **Yield:** 4 servings

Ingredients

- 1 avocado - peeled, pitted, and mashed
- ½ (15 ounce) can black beans, drained and rinsed
- 1 tablespoon lime juice
- 1 clove garlic, minced, or more to taste
- ⅓ cup shredded Cheddar cheese
- 1 pinch sea salt to taste

Directions

- **Step 1**

  Mix avocado, black beans, lime juice, and garlic together in a microwave-safe bowl. Sprinkle with Cheddar cheese.
- **Step 2**

  Microwave dip on high until cheese is melted, about 1 minute. Season with sea salt if desired.

Nutrition Facts

Per Serving:

177.1 calories; protein 7.1g 14% DV; carbohydrates 13.8g 5% DV; fat 11.3g 17% DV; cholesterol 12.1mg 4% DV; sodium 359.1mg 14% DV.

Easy Microwave Peanut Brittle

Prep: 10 mins **Cook:** 8 mins **Total:** 18 mins **Servings:** 6 **Yield:** 6 servings

Ingredients

- 1 serving cooking spray
- 1 cup white sugar
- ½ cup light corn syrup
- 1 ½ cups peanuts, or more to taste
- 1 tablespoon butter
- 1 teaspoon baking soda

- 1 teaspoon vanilla extract

Directions

- **Step 1**
  Spray a baking sheet and a wooden spoon with cooking spray.
- **Step 2**
  Mix sugar and corn syrup together in a microwaveable bowl safe for high temperatures.
- **Step 3**
  Heat sugar mixture in microwave on high for 5 minutes.
- **Step 4**
  Stir peanuts and butter into sugar mixture. Heat in microwave until mixture becomes a caramel color, 3 to 4 minutes.
- **Step 5**
  Mix baking soda and vanilla extract into syrup until smooth and foam has dissipated. Spread candy onto the prepared baking sheet using the sprayed wooden spoon. Work quickly; candy hardens fast. Let stand until cool. Break into pieces to serve.

Nutrition Facts

Per Serving:

439.3 calories; protein 8.7g 17% DV; carbohydrates 62.3g 20% DV; fat 20.1g 31% DV; cholesterol 5.1mg 2% DV; sodium 537.1mg 22% DV.

Easy Brownie In A Mug

Prep: 5 mins **Cook:** 5 mins **Total:** 10 mins **Servings:** 1 **Yield:** 1 brownie

Ingredients

- ¼ cup all-purpose flour
- ¼ cup white sugar
- 2 tablespoons cocoa powder
- 1 pinch ground cinnamon
- 1 pinch salt
- ¼ cup water
- 2 tablespoons canola oil
- 1 splash vanilla extract

Directions

- **Step 1**
  Stir flour, sugar, cocoa powder, cinnamon, and salt together in a microwave-safe mug. Stir water, oil, and vanilla extract into flour mixture with a fork until smooth.

- **Step 2**
  Microwave until set, 1 to 5 minutes.

Cook's Notes:

Do not use extra-virgin olive oil in place of vegetable/canola oil. Hot chocolate powder mix works in place of cocoa as well.

Nutrition Facts

Per Serving:

587.7 calories; protein 5.4g 11% DV; carbohydrates 80.8g 26% DV; fat 29.8g 46% DV; cholesterolmg; sodium 160mg 6% DV.

Super Simple Perfect Chocolate Ganache

Prep: 10 mins **Cook:** 1 min **Additional:** 25 mins **Total:** 36 mins **Servings:** 24 **Yield:** 1 1/2 cups

Ingredients

- ¾ cup heavy whipping cream
- 1 cup semisweet chocolate chips

Directions

- **Step 1**
  Pour cream into a microwave-safe bowl; heat in microwave on high until very hot, 1 to 2 minutes. Add chocolate chips to heated cream; whisk until smooth.
- **Step 2**
  Place chocolate-cream mixture in the freezer until ganache is cold and starting to thicken, stirring every 5 minutes, about 10 to 12 minutes.
- **Step 3**
  Spoon ganache into a resealable plastic bag and refrigerate until completely cooled, 15 to 30 minutes.
- **Step 4**
  Cut a corner from the plastic bag and pipe ganache.

Cook's Note:

Do not worry if mixture remains thin until cool. It will thicken. Some freezers will take longer.

Nutrition Facts

Per Serving:

59.2 calories; protein 0.4g 1% DV; carbohydrates 4.6g 2% DV; fat 4.9g 8% DV; cholesterol 10.2mg 3% DV; sodium 3.6mg.

Microwave Spiced Nuts

Prep: 5 mins **Cook:** 7 mins **Total:** 12 mins **Servings:** 12 **Yield:** 3 cups

Ingredients

- ¼ cup butter
- ½ cup brown sugar
- ½ teaspoon ground nutmeg
- 1 teaspoon ground cinnamon
- 2 tablespoons water
- 3 cups pecan halves

Directions

- **Step 1**

  Melt butter in a 4 quart glass casserole dish in the microwave. Stir in the brown sugar, nutmeg, cinnamon and water. Microwave on high for 1 minute. Stir in the nuts so they are well coated. Microwave for 4 to 5 additional minutes on high, stirring every minute. Spread cooked nuts out onto parchment or waxed paper to cool.

Nutrition Facts

Per Serving:

244.6 calories; protein 2.5g 5% DV; carbohydrates 9.9g 3% DV; fat 23.3g 36% DV; cholesterol 10.2mg 3% DV; sodium 29mg 1% DV.

Brownie In a Mug

Prep: 5 mins **Cook:** 2 mins **Total:** 7 mins **Servings:** 1 **Yield:** 1 brownie

Ingredients

- ¼ cup white sugar
- ¼ cup all-purpose flour
- 2 tablespoons cocoa powder
- 1 pinch salt
- 3 tablespoons water
- 2 tablespoons olive oil

Directions

- **Step 1**

  Stir sugar, flour, cocoa powder, and salt together in a mug. Add water and olive oil; stir until mixture is evenly moist.
- **Step 2**

  Cook in microwave for 1 minute 40 seconds. Serve topped with ice cream.

Nutrition Facts

Per Serving:

570.7 calories; protein 5.3g 11% DV; carbohydrates 79.7g 26% DV; fat 28.8g 44% DV; cholesterolmg; sodium 4.8mg.

Mayan Hot Chocolate

Prep: 5 mins **Cook:** 2 mins **Total:** 7 mins **Servings:** 1 **Yield:** 1 serving

Ingredients

- 1 cup milk
- 3 tablespoons instant hot chocolate mix
- 1 teaspoon ground cinnamon
- 1 pinch cayenne pepper

Directions

- **Step 1**
  Mix the hot chocolate mix, cinnamon, and cayenne pepper together in a mug.
- **Step 2**
  Pour the milk into a glass measuring cup; heat in microwave on High until it begins to boil, about 2 minutes. Slowly pour over the mixture in the mug, stirring with a small whisk as you pour. Enjoy immediately.

Tips

Snag a top-rated measuring cup for yourself using our guide to the best measuring cups, then get cooking with our favorite recipes.

Nutrition Facts

Per Serving:

223.8 calories; protein 9.8g 20% DV; carbohydrates 33.5g 11% DV; fat 5.8g 9% DV; cholesterol 19.5mg 7% DV; sodium 221.3mg 9% DV.

Chocolate Shell Sauce

Cook: 10 mins **Total:** 10 mins **Servings:** 4 **Yield:** 4 servings

Ingredients

- 3 tablespoons butter
- .66 cup semisweet chocolate chips

Directions

- **Step 1**
  Melt butter and chocolate in a small saucepan over medium heat, or in the microwave. Stirring frequently. Serve over ice cream.

Nutrition Facts

Per Serving:

209.1 calories; protein 1.3g 3% DV; carbohydrates 17.5g 6% DV; fat 17g 26% DV; cholesterol 22.9mg 8% DV; sodium 64.4mg 3% DV.

Cheesy Cauliflower in the Microwave

Prep: 10 mins **Cook:** 15 mins **Total:** 25 mins **Servings:** 4 **Yield:** 4 servings

Ingredients

- 1 medium head cauliflower, separated into florets
- 1 serving butter-flavored cooking spray (such as I Can't Believe It's Not Butter)
- ¼ teaspoon salt, or to taste
- ⅛ teaspoon ground black pepper
- ¼ cup Italian-style bread crumbs
- ¼ cup freshly grated Parmesan cheese
- 3 cloves garlic, minced, or more to taste
- ¼ teaspoon red pepper flakes

Directions

- **Step 1**
  Place cauliflower in a microwave-safe bowl and cover with paper towels. Cook in the microwave on high for 5 to 6 minutes. Remove from the microwave, drain any liquid, and stir cauliflower. Return to the microwave and cook until soft, 5 to 6 more minutes.
- **Step 2**
  Spray cauliflower with butter-flavored cooking spray and season with salt and pepper. Sprinkle with bread crumbs, Parmesan cheese, and garlic; stir to combine.
- **Step 3**
  Microwave until cheese is melted, 1 to 2 more minutes.

Nutrition Facts

Per Serving:

82.1 calories; protein 5.3g 11% DV; carbohydrates 12.1g 4% DV; fat 2g 3% DV; cholesterol 4.4mg 2% DV; sodium 363.8mg 15% DV.

Easy, Fast Chocolate Cup Muffin

Cook: 5 mins **Total:** 5 mins **Servings:** 1 **Yield:** 1 serving

Ingredients

- 1 egg
- 1 ½ tablespoons all-purpose flour
- 1 tablespoon melted butter
- 1 tablespoon baking cocoa
- ½ tablespoon white sugar

Directions

- **Step 1**
  Combine egg, flour, melted butter, cocoa, and sugar in a large microwave-safe cup and mix thoroughly. Cook in the microwave for about 2 minutes.

Nutrition Facts

Per Serving:

252.5 calories; protein 8.7g 17% DV; carbohydrates 18.5g 6% DV; fat 17.3g 27% DV; cholesterol 216.5mg 72% DV; sodium 153.2mg 6% DV.

Candied Acorn Squash

Prep: 5 mins **Cook:** 10 mins **Total:** 15 mins **Servings:** 4 **Yield:** 4 servings

Ingredients

- 1 acorn squash, halved and seeded
- ¼ cup butter, divided
- ¼ cup packed brown sugar, divided

Directions

- **Step 1**
  Place both halves of the squash cut side up on a microwave-safe plate or dish. Put 2 tablespoons of butter, and 2 tablespoons of brown sugar into the cavity of each half.
- **Step 2**
  Cook for 8 to 10 minutes in the microwave on full power. Rotate the squash a couple of times to ensure even cooking. When the flesh is soft, scoop out soft flesh with the sugar and butter, and place it in a bowl. Mash it a little to blend the ingredients. Serve in a bowl, or your could even serve it in the shells.

Nutrition Facts

Per Serving:

204 calories; protein 1.1g 2% DV; carbohydrates 26.5g 9% DV; fat 11.6g 18% DV; cholesterol 30.5mg 10% DV; sodium 89.3mg 4% DV.

Apple Butter the Easy Way Microwave Macaroni and Cheese

Prep: 10 mins **Cook:** 10 mins **Additional:** 5 mins **Total:** 25 mins **Servings:** 4 **Yield:** 4 servings

Ingredients

- 8 ounces macaroni
- 2 tablespoons butter
- 2 ½ tablespoons chopped onion
- 16 ounces cubed processed cheese food
- ¾ cup milk
- salt to taste
- ground black pepper to taste

Directions

- **Step 1**
  In a large pot with boiling salted water cook the elbow macaroni until al dente. Drain and set aside.
- **Step 2**
  In a 2-quart microwave-safe covered casserole dish, cook the onions and butter or margarine on high for 3 to 4 minutes.
- **Step 3**
  Add the cooked and drained pasta, milk, and cubed cheese and stir. Cook for 11 to 12 minutes on high, stirring well after 4, 8, and 11 minutes. The mixture will still be runny at this stage. Add salt and pepper to taste.
- **Step 4**
  Let stand for 5-8 minutes before serving. The sauce will thicken as it cools slightly.

Nutrition Facts

Per Serving:

659.4 calories; protein 31.2g 63% DV; carbohydrates 54g 17% DV; fat 35.2g 54% DV; cholesterol 91.5mg 31% DV; sodium 1158.7mg 46% DV.

Chocolate Covered Blueberries

Prep: 10 mins **Cook:** 5 mins **Total:** 15 mins **Servings:** 36 **Yield:** 36 candies

Ingredients

- 1 cup semi-sweet chocolate chips
- 1 tablespoon shortening
- 2 cups fresh blueberries, rinsed and dried

Directions

- **Step 1**
  Melt chocolate in a glass bowl in the microwave, or in a metal bowl set over a pan of simmering water. Stir frequently until melted and smooth. Remove from the heat, and stir in the shortening until melted.
- **Step 2**
  Line a baking sheet with waxed paper. Add blueberries to the chocolate, and stir gently to coat. Spoon small clumps of blueberries onto the waxed paper. Refrigerate until firm, about 10 minutes. Store in a cool place in an airtight container. These will last about 2 days.

Nutrition Facts

Per Serving:

30.1 calories; protein 0.3g 1% DV; carbohydrates 4.1g 1% DV; fat 1.8g 3% DV; cholesterolmg; sodium 0.6mg.

Celery Salt

Prep: 5 mins **Cook:** 1 min **Additional:** 10 mins **Total:** 16 mins **Servings:** 12 **Yield:** 1 /4 cup celery salt

Ingredients

- ½ cup loosely-packed celery leaves, cut into 1-inch pieces
- ¼ cup kosher salt

Directions

- **Step 1**
  Line a microwave-safe plate with a paper towel. Place celery leaves in a single layer and cover with a second paper towel. Microwave leaves, rearranging if needed, in 30-second intervals until dry and crispy. Uncover and cool, about 10 minutes.
- **Step 2**
  Measure out 2 tablespoons of dried leaves and crumble with your fingers. Add to salt and mix well. Briefly pulse in a spice grinder if desired.

Cook's Note:

Substitute sea salt for the kosher salt if desired.

Do not use recycled paper towels, as they may catch on fire!

The celery leaves may be dried until crisp in an oven set at the lowest possible temperature, instead of in a microwave.

Nutrition Facts

Per Serving:

0.8 calories; proteing; carbohydrates 0.2g; fatg; cholesterolmg; sodium 1901.9mg 76% DV.

Mom's Goulash in the Microwave

Prep: 10 mins **Cook:** 25 mins **Total:** 35 mins **Servings:** 6 **Yield:** 6 servings

Ingredients

- 1 (8 ounce) package uncooked elbow macaroni
- 1 pound ground beef
- 1 cup diced onion
- 1 cup sliced celery
- 1 tablespoon minced garlic
- 1 (14.5 ounce) can diced tomatoes
- 1 (10 ounce) can tomato sauce
- 1 tablespoon sugar
- 1 tablespoon paprika
- 1 teaspoon dried oregano
- ¼ teaspoon caraway seed
- 1 pinch cayenne pepper, or to taste

- 1 teaspoon salt

Directions

- **Step 1**

  Bring a pot of lightly salted water to a boil. Add the macaroni, and cook until tender, about 8 minutes. Drain.
- **Step 2**

  Meanwhile, crumble the ground beef into a 2 quart or larger casserole dish. Add the onion, celery and garlic. Cook in the microwave on High for 5 to 6 minutes, or until beef is no longer pink. Stir once during cooking. Drain off the grease.
- **Step 3**

  Stir the tomatoes, tomato sauce and sugar into the beef, and season with paprika, oregano, caraway seed, cayenne pepper and salt. Cover, and cook in the microwave on power level 8 for about 14 minutes, or until celery is tender and the flavors have blended.
- **Step 4**

  Remove from the microwave, and mix in the cooked macaroni. Cook for 2 to 3 more minutes, until heated through. Serve.

Nutrition Facts

Per Serving:

326.7 calories; protein 19.4g 39% DV; carbohydrates 39.2g 13% DV; fat 9.8g 15% DV; cholesterol 45.9mg 15% DV; sodium 802.7mg 32% DV.

10-Minute Chocolate Mug Cake

Prep: 5 mins **Cook:** 2 mins **Total:** 7 mins **Servings:** 1 **Yield:** 1 cake

Ingredients

- 5 tablespoons white sugar
- ¼ cup all-purpose flour
- 3 tablespoons milk
- 3 tablespoons olive oil
- 2 tablespoons unsweetened cocoa powder
- 1 egg
- 1 dash pure vanilla extract
- 1 pinch salt

Directions

- **Step 1**

  Mix sugar, flour, milk, olive oil, cocoa powder, egg, vanilla extract, and salt together in a large microwave-safe mug.

- **Step 2**
  Heat in microwave until center of cake is done, about 2 minutes.

Cook's Note:

Because this recipe makes such a big mug cake, split the batter in two for a smaller cake. Microwave for 1 minute to 1 minute 50 seconds or until a tooth pick comes out clean. If the edges of the cake begin to bubble take out of microwave immediately.

Substitute 4 teaspoons stevia extract for the sugar, if desired.

Substitute vegetable oil for the olive oil, if desired.

Nutrition Facts

Per Serving:

835.6 calories; protein 13.1g 26% DV; carbohydrates 94.9g 31% DV; fat 48.2g 74% DV; cholesterol 189.7mg 63% DV; sodium 247.6mg 10% DV.

Gaye's Microwave Fudge

Prep: 3 mins **Cook:** 2 mins **Additional:** 10 mins **Total:** 15 mins **Servings:** 12 **Yield:** 1 - 9x9 inch dish

Ingredients

- 4 cups confectioners' sugar
- ½ cup unsweetened cocoa powder
- ¼ cup milk
- ½ cup butter
- 2 teaspoons vanilla extract

Directions

- **Step 1**
  Grease a 9x9 inch dish.
- **Step 2**
  In a microwave safe bowl, stir together confectioners' sugar and cocoa. Pour milk over mixture and place butter in bowl. Do not mix. Microwave until butter is melted, 2 minutes. Stir in vanilla and stir vigorously until smooth. Pour into prepared dish.
- **Step 3**
  Chill in freezer 10 minutes before cutting into squares.

Nutrition Facts

Per Serving:

243.2 calories; protein 1g 2% DV; carbohydrates 43.9g 14% DV; fat 8.3g 13% DV; cholesterol 20.7mg 7% DV; sodium 57.8mg 2% DV.

PB and J Mini Mug Cakes

Prep: 10 mins **Cook:** 5 mins **Total:** 15 mins **Servings:** 4 **Yield:** 4 mug cakes

Ingredients

- 4 servings cooking spray (such as Pam)
- 4 teaspoons Concord grape jelly
- ½ cup yellow cake mix
- 2 tablespoons creamy peanut butter (such as Peter Pan)
- 2 cups whipped cream (such as Reddi-Whip)
- ¼ cup egg substitute (such as Egg Beaters)

Directions

- **Step 1**
  Spray the insides of 4 microwave-safe mugs with cooking spray.
- **Step 2**
  Spoon 1 teaspoon grape jelly into the bottom of each mug.
- **Step 3**
  Whisk cake mix and peanut butter together in a bowl; add whipped cream and egg substitute and whisk until batter is smooth. Divide batter evenly between the mugs.
- **Step 4**
  Place 1 mug in the microwave and cook on high until cake is set, about 1 minute, 15 seconds. Repeat with remaining mugs. Invert each mug onto a plate to release cakes.

Nutrition Facts

Per Serving:

230 calories; protein 5.6g 11% DV; carbohydrates 22.9g 7% DV; fat 13.5g 21% DV; cholesterol 23.3mg 8% DV; sodium 215mg 9% DV.

S'more Pie

Prep: 15 mins **Cook:** 40 mins **Additional:** 15 mins **Total:** 1 hr 10 mins **Servings:** 12 **Yield:** 1 pie

Ingredients

Crust:

- 1 ½ cups graham cracker crumbs
- ¼ cup butter, melted
- ¼ cup white sugar
- ¼ teaspoon salt

Graham Brownie:

- 2 cups graham cracker crumbs
- 1 (14 ounce) can condensed milk
- ½ cup semisweet chocolate chips
- 1 teaspoon baking powder
- ⅛ teaspoon salt

Chocolate Custard:

- ¾ cup white sugar
- 5 tablespoons cocoa powder
- 3 tablespoons cornstarch
- ¼ teaspoon salt
- 2 cups milk
- 1 egg, beaten
- 1 teaspoon vanilla extract
- 2 cups regular marshmallows
- 1 cup miniature marshmallows

Chocolate Ganache:

- ¼ cup heavy cream
- ¼ cup chopped semisweet chocolate
- ½ teaspoon butter
- ¼ teaspoon instant coffee granules

Directions

- **Step 1**
  Preheat the oven to 350 degrees F (175 degrees C).
- **Step 2**
  Mix together graham cracker crumbs, melted butter, sugar, and salt for the crust, and press into the bottom of a springform pan.
- **Step 3**
  Mix graham cracker crumbs, condensed milk, chocolate chips, baking powder, and salt for the graham brownie in a large bowl until well combined. Gently spread on top of graham cracker crust.
- **Step 4**
  Bake in the preheated oven until top is dry, about 30 minutes. Remove pie from the oven and set aside to cool slightly. Increase oven temperature to 425 degrees F (220 degrees C).
- **Step 5**
  Meanwhile, whisk together sugar, cocoa powder, cornstarch and salt for the chocolate custard in a saucepan. Gradually whisk in milk. Cook and stir over medium-high heat until thickened, 5 to 7 minutes. Reduce heat to medium-low and cook for about 2 minutes more. Pour beaten egg gradually into the chocolate custard, stirring as you pour. Cook and stir for 2 minutes. Remove from the heat and stir in vanilla extract.
- **Step 6**
  Pour chocolate custard over the baked pie. Arrange regular marshmallows on top of the pie and sprinkle miniature marshmallows to fill in any gaps.
- **Step 7**

Bake until marshmallows are lightly browned, about 5 minutes; keep an eye on it because you do not want marshmallows to melt.

- **Step 8**
  Place cream for chocolate ganache in a microwave-safe bowl. Microwave on High until hot, making sure it doesn't bubble over, about 45 seconds to 1 minute. Mix in chocolate, butter, and coffee granules. Microwave for another 30 seconds then stir until smooth. Let sit until it thickens, 15 to 20 minutes. Drizzle chocolate ganache over the pie.

Cook's Note:

If you have a torch, use that to brown the marshmallows instead of the oven.

Nutrition Facts

Per Serving:

453.8 calories; protein 7.5g 15% DV; carbohydrates 74g 24% DV; fat 16.2g 25% DV; cholesterol 45.4mg 15% DV; sodium 417.6mg 17% DV.

Sweet Sticky Rice with Mangoes

Prep: 15 mins **Cook:** 20 mins **Additional:** 1 hr **Total:** 1 hr 35 mins **Servings:** 6 **Yield:** 6 servings

Ingredients

- 2 cups uncooked glutinous (sticky) white rice, rinsed
- 1 (13.5 ounce) can coconut milk, divided
- 1 cup white sugar
- 1 tablespoon white sugar
- ¼ teaspoon salt
- ¾ teaspoon cornstarch
- 2 eaches ripe mangoes, peeled and cubed

Directions

- **Step 1**
  Cover the rice with several inches of fresh water. Allow rice to stand for 30 minutes. Drain off water so that rice is covered by 1/4 inch of water.
- **Step 2**
  Place the rice in a microwave oven, cover, and cook on High until the water has mostly absorbed but the rice is still wet, about 10 minutes; stir and cook until almost dry, an additional 4 minutes.
- **Step 3**
  Mix half the coconut milk and 1 cup of sugar in a bowl, stirring to dissolve the sugar. Pour the mixture over the rice and stir to coat rice with the mixture. Cover and allow the rice to stand at room temperature for 20 minutes.
- **Step 4**

Pour the remaining 1/2 can of coconut milk into a saucepan and whisk in 1 tablespoon of sugar, salt, and cornstarch until smooth. Bring the mixture to a simmer over medium heat, whisking constantly, and simmer until thickened, about 2 minutes. Remove from heat and allow to cool.

- **Step 5**

  To serve, scoop the rice into individual serving bowls and top each serving with about 2 tablespoons of the coconut sauce and several pieces of mango.

Cook's Note:

You can also steam the sweet rice using the traditional method. You may want to leave the salt out and taste the sauce before you add any.

Nutrition Facts

Per Serving:

525.1 calories; protein 5.7g 12% DV; carbohydrates 96.4g 31% DV; fat 14.1g 22% DV; cholesterolmg; sodium 110.6mg 4% DV.

Creamy Chicken Tortilla Bake

Prep: 15 mins **Cook:** 15 mins **Total:** 30 mins **Servings:** 8 **Yield:** 8 servings

Ingredients

- 1 tablespoon butter
- ½ cup chopped onion
- 1 (10.75 ounce) can condensed cream of chicken soup
- 1 cup sour cream
- ¼ teaspoon ground cumin
- 8 (6 inch) corn tortillas
- 2 (4 ounce) cans chopped green chiles, drained
- 3 cups cubed, cooked chicken
- 1 (8 ounce) package shredded Cheddar cheese
- 1 (8 ounce) package shredded Monterey Jack cheese

Directions

- **Step 1**

  Melt butter in a large skillet over medium heat; cook and stir onion until tender and translucent, about 5 minutes. Mix in cream of chicken soup, sour cream, and cumin.

- **Step 2**

  Grease a 9x12-inch microwave-safe baking dish and place 4 tortillas in a layer into the bottom of the dish. Top with 1 can green chilies, half the chicken, half the soup mix, half the Cheddar cheese, and half the Monterey Jack cheese. Repeat layers, ending with Monterey Jack cheese.

- **Step 3**

  Cook in microwave oven on high until the casserole is bubbling and the cheese topping is melted, about 10 minutes.

Nutrition Facts

Per Serving:

507.6 calories; protein 30.5g 61% DV; carbohydrates 18.5g 6% DV; fat 34.8g 54% DV; cholesterol 114.8mg 38% DV; sodium 975mg 39% DV.

The Best Steamed Asparagus

Prep: 3 mins **Cook:** 3 mins **Additional:** 5 mins **Total:** 11 mins **Servings:** 4 **Yield:** 4 servings

Ingredients

- 1 pound fresh asparagus spears, trimmed
- ¼ cup white wine
- 2 tablespoons butter

Directions

- **Step 1**

  Place asparagus in a microwave-safe dish. Pour in wine, and dot with pieces of butter.
- **Step 2**

  Cover loosely, and cook in the microwave on High for 3 minutes, or until bright green and tender. Allow the dish to stand 5 minutes before serving.

Nutrition Facts

Per Serving:

86.4 calories; protein 2.6g 5% DV; carbohydrates 4.8g 2% DV; fat 5.9g 9% DV; cholesterol 15.3mg 5% DV; sodium 43.9mg 2% DV.

Easy Egg White Omelet

Prep: 10 mins **Cook:** 10 mins **Total:** 20 mins **Servings:** 4 **Yield:** 4 servings

Ingredients

- 1 serving cooking spray
- 2 tablespoons chopped onion
- 2 tablespoons chopped green bell pepper
- 2 tablespoons chopped mushrooms
- 1 pinch salt and ground black pepper to taste
- 1 (32 ounce) container refrigerated pasteurized egg white substitute (such as Egg Beaters Whites)

Directions

- **Step 1**

  Spray a 9x5-inch glass or microwave-safe loaf pan with cooking spray; sprinkle the onion, green bell pepper, and mushrooms into the pan, and toss lightly with a fork just to mix. Season with salt and black pepper, and pour in the egg whites.
- **Step 2**

Cook in a microwave oven on High setting for 3 minutes. Remove and stir the cooked egg white from the side of the pan into the rest of the ingredients; cook for 3 more minutes on High. If the omelet is still a little runny on top, slice it into chunks and turn them over in the loaf pan; microwave for 30 more seconds on High. Adjust salt and pepper, and serve.

Nutrition Facts

Per Serving:

127.7 calories; protein 24.9g 50% DV; carbohydrates 0.8g; fat 0.1g; cholesterolmg; sodium 370.9mg 15% DV.

Microwave Cake

Servings: 12 **Yield:** 12 servings

Ingredients

- 1 (18.25 ounce) package yellow cake mix
- 3 large eggs eggs
- 1 (21 ounce) can apple pie filling
- ½ cup applesauce

Directions

- **Step 1**
  Mix the box of cake mix, eggs, pie filling and applesauce till moist. Use a microwave safe bundt pan or substitute a microwave safe bowl that has a microwave safe cup or cone placed in the middle of it (to mimic a bundt pan). Pour mixture into the bowl around the cup.
- **Step 2**
  Bake on high for 6 minutes 30 seconds, turn and bake for another 6 minutes 30 seconds on high. Remove from oven and cover bowl with a dish and let stand for 5 minutes (this finishes the cooking process).
- **Step 3**
  Turn cake over onto dish and remove cone (cup) for a delicious quick dessert. Good hot with vanilla ice cream or whipped topping.

Nutrition Facts

Per Serving:

258.4 calories; protein 3.5g 7% DV; carbohydrates 47.9g 15% DV; fat 6.3g 10% DV; cholesterol 47.4mg 16% DV; sodium 322.6mg 13% DV.

Crispy Peanut Butter Chocolate Log

Prep: 15 mins **Cook:** 5 mins **Additional:** 1 hr **Total:** 1 hr 20 mins **Servings:** 12 **Yield:** 12 servings

Ingredients

- 1 (10 ounce) package large marshmallows

- ¼ cup butter
- ¼ cup peanut butter
- 5 ½ cups crispy rice cereal (such as Rice Krispies)
- 1 ⅓ cups semi-sweet chocolate chips
- ¾ cup butterscotch chips

Directions

- **Step 1**
  Line a 15x10x1-inch pan with waxed paper. Grease the waxed paper.
- **Step 2**
  Combine marshmallows, butter, and peanut butter together in a large microwave-safe bowl. Cover bowl and heat mixture in the microwave until marshmallows are melted, about 2 minutes. Stir well.
- **Step 3**
  Stir rice cereal into marshmallow mixture until well coated; spread onto the prepared pan.
- **Step 4**
  Combine chocolate chips and butterscotch chips in a microwave-safe bowl. Heat mixture in microwave until melted, about 2 minutes. Stir well.
- **Step 5**
  Spread chocolate mixture over rice cereal mixture, leaving a 1-inch border around edges. Roll rice cereal mixture around chocolate filling, jelly-roll style and starting with the short side. Peel waxed paper away while rolling. Place roll, seam-side down, on a serving platter. Refrigerate until set, about 1 hour. Cut into narrow slices.

Nutrition Facts

Per Serving:

337.7 calories; protein 3.5g 7% DV; carbohydrates 50g 16% DV; fat 15.4g 24% DV; cholesterol 10.2mg 3% DV; sodium 182.2mg 7% DV.

Prep: 10 mins **Cook:** 20 mins **Total:** 30 mins **Servings:** 16 **Yield:** 16 servings

Ingredients

- 2 pounds chopped apples
- ⅓ cup maple syrup
- ½ teaspoon ground cinnamon

Directions

- **Step 1**
- In a microwave safe bowl, combine apples, maple syrup and cinnamon. Microwave on high for 15 minutes. Transfer mixture to a blender and process until smooth. Return mixture to bowl and microwave 5 minutes more. Cool and transfer to a jar. Store in refrigerator.

Nutrition Facts

Per Serving:

46.8 calories; protein 0.2g; carbohydrates 12.3g 4% DV; fat 0.1g; cholesterolmg; sodium 1.2mg.

Jalapeno Chicken Dip

Prep: 5 mins **Cook:** 5 mins **Total:** 10 mins **Servings:** 15 **Yield:** 15 servings

Ingredients

- 1 (10 ounce) can chunk white chicken in water, thoroughly drained
- 1 pinch seasoned salt
- 2 (8 ounce) packages cream cheese, softened
- 1 (10.75 ounce) can condensed cream of chicken soup
- 3 tablespoons chopped jalapeno

Directions

- **Step 1**
  Combine the chicken and seasoned salt in a large skillet over medium-low heat; heat through.
- **Step 2**
  Combine the cream cheese and chicken soup in a microwave-safe bowl; cover and heat for 1 minute in the microwave. Add the chicken mixture and continue to heat at 1 minute intervals until the liquid bubbles. Stir in the jalapenos and serve immediately.

Nutrition Facts

Per Serving:

153.8 calories; protein 6.8g 14% DV; carbohydrates 2.3g 1% DV; fat 13.1g 20% DV; cholesterol 46.1mg 15% DV; sodium 330.8mg 13% DV.

Microwave Pralines

Prep: 9 mins **Cook:** 9 mins **Total:** 18 mins **Servings:** 36 **Yield:** 3 dozen

Ingredients

- 1 ½ cups brown sugar
- .66 cup heavy cream
- ⅛ teaspoon salt
- 2 tablespoons margarine
- 1 ½ cups pecan halves
- 1 teaspoon vanilla extract

Directions

- **Step 1**
  In a large, microwave safe bowl, combine sugar, cream, salt, margarine and pecans. Microwave 9 minutes on high, stirring once. Let rest 1 minute. Stir in vanilla and continue to stir 3 minutes more.

Drop by teaspoonfuls onto buttered waxed paper. (If mixture is runny, allow to cool 30 seconds more and try again.)

Nutrition Facts

Per Serving:

86.6 calories; protein 0.5g 1% DV; carbohydrates 9.8g 3% DV; fat 5.4g 8% DV; cholesterol 6mg 2% DV; sodium 19.2mg 1% DV.

Chocolaty Peanut Butter Haystacks

Prep: 10 mins **Cook:** 5 mins **Additional:** 20 mins **Total:** 35 mins **Servings:** 30 **Yield:** 30 servings

Ingredients

- 1 cup semi-sweet chocolate chips
- ⅓ cup peanut butter
- ½ cup toffee baking bits (such as Heath)
- 1 cup chow mein noodles

Directions

- **Step 1**
  Place the chocolate chips into a microwave-safe bowl and cook on High for 30 seconds; stir and repeat several times, just until the chips are melted. Add peanut butter, cook for 20 more seconds to warm the peanut butter, and mix thoroughly. Mix in the toffee bits and chow mein noodles; stir to coat the ingredients with the chocolate mixture.
- **Step 2**
  Line a baking sheet with parchment or waxed paper; drop the mixture onto the lined sheets by the tablespoon. Refrigerate until set.

Nutrition Facts

Per Serving:

75.9 calories; protein 1.2g 3% DV; carbohydrates 7.4g 2% DV; fat 5g 8% DV; cholesterol 3.3mg 1% DV; sodium 39.4mg 2% DV.

Brown Rice, Broccoli, Cheese and Walnut Surprise

Prep: 15 mins **Cook:** 25 mins **Total:** 40 mins **Servings:** 4 **Yield:** 4 servings

Ingredients

- ½ cup chopped walnuts
- 1 tablespoon butter
- 1 onion, chopped
- ½ teaspoon minced garlic
- 1 cup uncooked instant brown rice

- 1 cup vegetable broth
- 1 pound fresh broccoli florets
- ½ teaspoon salt
- ⅛ teaspoon ground black pepper
- 1 cup shredded Cheddar cheese

Directions

- **Step 1**
  Preheat oven to 350 degrees F (175 degrees C). Place walnuts on small baking sheet, and bake for 6 to 8 minutes or until toasted.
- **Step 2**
  Melt butter in a medium saucepan over medium heat. Cook onion and garlic in melted butter for 3 minutes, stirring frequently. Stir in the rice, add the broth, and bring to a boil. Reduce heat to medium-low. Cover, and simmer until liquid is absorbed, about 7 to 8 minutes.
- **Step 3**
  Place broccoli in a microwave-safe casserole dish, and sprinkle with salt and pepper. Cover, and microwave until tender.
- **Step 4**
  Spoon rice onto a serving platter, and top with broccoli. Sprinkle walnuts and cheese on top.

Nutrition Facts

Per Serving:

367.7 calories; protein 15.1g 30% DV; carbohydrates 30.4g 10% DV; fat 22.9g 35% DV; cholesterol 37.3mg 12% DV; sodium 643mg 26% DV.

Twice-Baked Ranch Potatoes

Prep: 10 mins **Cook:** 25 mins **Additional:** 10 mins **Total:** 45 mins **Servings:** 5 **Yield:** 5 servings

Ingredients

- 5 (5 ounce) baking potatoes
- 4 ounces Neufchatel cheese, softened
- 2 tablespoons milk
- 1 (1 ounce) package ranch salad dressing mix
- ½ cup shredded reduced-fat Cheddar cheese

Directions

- **Step 1**
  Scrub and dry potatoes, then prick several times with a fork and place on a microwave-safe plate. Heat in microwave on high until tender, 18 to 20 minutes; remove and allow to cool for 10 minutes.
- **Step 2**
  Combine Neufchatel cheese and milk in a small bowl; beat in salad dressing mix.

- **Step 3**
  Cut potatoes in half lengthwise; remove pulp, leaving a thin potato skin shell. Mix pulp into cheese mixture and mash. Spoon mixture into potato shells; sprinkle with Cheddar cheese.
- **Step 4**
  Place two potatoes on a microwave-safe plate. Heat in microwave on high until heated through and cheese is melted, 3 1/2 to 4 1/2 minutes.

Nutrition Facts

Per Serving:

204.9 calories; protein 8.1g 16% DV; carbohydrates 28.8g 9% DV; fat 6.4g 10% DV; cholesterol 20.1mg 7% DV; sodium 562.7mg 23% DV.

Chocolate Ice Cream Mug Cake

Prep: 5 mins **Cook:** 2 mins **Total:** 7 mins **Servings:** 1 **Yield:** 1 serving

Ingredients

- ⅓ cup vanilla ice cream, melted
- 1 ½ tablespoons all-purpose flour
- ¼ teaspoon baking powder
- 1 teaspoon unsweetened cocoa powder
- 1 scoop vanilla ice cream

Directions

- **Step 1**
  Mix melted ice cream, flour, and baking powder together in a microwave-safe mug. Stir in cocoa powder. Microwave until top of cake looks done, about 90 seconds. Top with vanilla ice cream.

Nutrition Facts

Per Serving:

178.3 calories; protein 3.9g 8% DV; carbohydrates 25.6g 8% DV; fat 7.5g 12% DV; cholesterol 28.6mg 10% DV; sodium 174.5mg 7% DV.

Mexican Chocolate/Salted Caramel Cake in a Mug

Prep: 10 mins **Cook:** 2 mins **Total:** 12 mins **Servings:** 1 **Yield:** 1 cake

Ingredients

- 2 tablespoons all-purpose flour
- 3 tablespoons white sugar
- 2 tablespoons unsweetened cocoa powder
- 2 tablespoons chocolate chips
- ¼ teaspoon baking powder
- 1 pinch salt
- 1 pinch cayenne pepper
- 1 pinch ground cinnamon
- 3 tablespoons milk
- 1 tablespoon canola oil
- 1 egg, beaten
- ½ teaspoon vanilla extract
- 2 caramels individually wrapped caramels, unwrapped and halved
- 1 pinch kosher salt

Directions

- **Step 1**
  Mix flour, sugar, cocoa powder, chocolate chips, baking powder, 1 pinch salt, cayenne pepper, and cinnamon in a bowl. Whisk milk, canola oil, egg, and vanilla extract together in a separate bowl; stir into flour mixture. Lightly press caramels into kosher salt.
- **Step 2**
  Pour batter into a microwave-safe mug; top with salted caramels.
- **Step 3**
  Cook in microwave until desired consistency is reached, 75 to 100 seconds.

Cook's Notes:

I mix up single servings and store in an airtight container for a quick snack. You can add wheat germ or flax seed to make it healthier (and you feel better about it). Also, try it with carob powder if you want.

Nutrition Facts

Per Serving:

632.6 calories; protein 13.4g 27% DV; carbohydrates 88.1g 28% DV; fat 29.5g 45% DV; cholesterol 191.1mg 64% DV; sodium 665.4mg 27% DV.

Microwave Vegetables

Prep: 5 mins **Cook:** 5 mins **Total:** 10 mins **Servings:** 6 **Yield:** 6 servings

Ingredients

- 1 red bell pepper, chopped
- 1 tablespoon extra-virgin olive oil
- 7 ounces frozen peas
- 1 (12 fluid ounce) can canned sweet corn, drained

- 1 teaspoon chopped fresh cilantro
- 1 pinch salt and pepper to taste

Directions

- **Step 1**
  Combine red bell pepper and olive oil in a microwave-safe bowl. Microwave at full power until softened, about 1 minute. Add peas and cook at full power for an additional 2 minutes. Add corn and cook for 1 more minute. Stir vegetables and microwave for 30 seconds more. Add cilantro and season with salt and pepper. Stir and serve immediately.

Nutrition Facts

Per Serving:

88.4 calories; protein 2.8g 6% DV; carbohydrates 14g 5% DV; fat 2.7g 4% DV; cholesterolmg; sodium 229.1mg 9% DV.

Simple Microwave Peanut Brittle

Prep: 10 mins **Cook:** 20 mins **Total:** 30 mins **Servings:** 32 **Yield:** 2 pounds

Ingredients

- 1 cup light corn syrup
- 2 cups white sugar
- ⅔ cup peanuts
- 2 tablespoons butter
- 2 teaspoons vanilla extract
- 2 teaspoons baking soda

Directions

- **Step 1**
  In a 3 quart casserole dish, combine the corn syrup, sugar and peanuts. Microwave on high for 12 minutes. Stir in butter and vanilla, cook on high for 4 minutes. Stir in baking soda.
- **Step 2**
  Pour onto buttered cookie sheet; cool and break into pieces.

Nutrition Facts

Per Serving:

102.3 calories; protein 0.7g 2% DV; carbohydrates 21.1g 7% DV; fat 2.2g 3% DV; cholesterol 1.9mg 1% DV; sodium 90.3mg 4% DV.

Lemon Drop Bark

Prep: 10 mins **Cook:** 2 mins **Additional:** 30 mins **Total:** 42 mins **Servings:** 12 **Yield:** 12 servings

Ingredients

- 1 (12 ounce) package white chocolate chips (such as Nestle)
- ¾ cup lemon drop candies (such as Brach's)

Directions

- **Step 1**
  Place white chocolate chips in a microwave-safe 2-cup measuring cup; heat in microwave until melted, about 2 minutes. Stir until smooth.

- **Step 2**
  Place lemon drop candies in a resealable plastic bag. Place this bag into another resealable bag, creating a double bag so the candies don't puncture the bag. Crack candies with rolling pin or mallet until broken into small pieces.
- **Step 3**
  Stir cracked candies into melted white chocolate. Smooth mixture onto a piece of aluminum foil to about 1/4-inch thickness. Chill in refrigerator until set, at least 30 minutes. Break bark into small pieces and store in an air-tight container in the refrigerator.

Nutrition Facts

Per Serving:

218.8 calories; protein 2g 4% DV; carbohydrates 30.7g 10% DV; fat 10g 15% DV; cholesterol 6mg 2% DV; sodium 35.6mg 1% DV.

Denny's Amazing Five Minute Asiago Dip

Prep: 4 mins **Cook:** 2 mins **Total:** 6 mins **Servings:** 8 **Yield:** 8 servings

Ingredients

- 1 cup grated Asiago cheese
- 1 cup mayonnaise
- 1 (6.5 ounce) jar marinated artichoke hearts, drained and chopped
- 1 clove garlic, minced

Directions

- **Step 1**
  In a microwave-safe bowl, stir together the Asiago cheese, mayonnaise, artichoke hears and garlic. Heat in the microwave at 50% power for 30 seconds at a time, stirring between heatings until cheese has melted and dip has a smooth consistency. Serve warm.

Nutrition Facts

Per Serving:

266.5 calories; protein 4.5g 9% DV; carbohydrates 3.4g 1% DV; fat 26.9g 41% DV; cholesterol 22.5mg 8% DV; sodium 405.5mg 16% DV.

Dill-Pickled Cherry Tomatoes

Prep: 10 mins **Cook:** 2 mins **Additional:** 1 week **Total:** 1 week **Servings:** 12 **Yield:** 1 quart

Ingredients

- 4 cups green cherry tomatoes
- 1 (1 quart) sterilized canning jar with lid and ring
- 1 cup distilled white vinegar
- 1 cup water
- 3 tablespoons kosher salt
- 1 tablespoon sriracha sauce
- 1 tablespoon pickling spice

Directions

- **Step 1**
  Pack tomatoes into the 1-quart jar.

- **Step 2**
  Combine vinegar, water, salt, sriracha sauce, and pickling spice in a glass measuring cup. Heat in the microwave until boiling and salt dissolves, 1 1/2 to 3 minutes. Pour over tomatoes in the jar; seal.
- **Step 3**
  Refrigerate until pickled, 1 to 2 weeks.

Nutrition Facts

Per Serving:

15.6 calories; protein 0.7g 1% DV; carbohydrates 3.3g 1% DV; fat 0.1g; cholesterolmg; sodium 1501.3mg 60% DV.

Scottish Pudding

Prep: 5 mins **Cook:** 10 mins **Total:** 15 mins **Servings:** 8 **Yield:** 8 servings

Ingredients

- 1 cup water
- ¾ cup white sugar
- 1 tablespoon mixed spice
- 1 tablespoon cinnamon
- 1 ¼ cups chopped mixed dried fruit
- 1 ¼ cups golden raisins
- 1 cup margarine
- 2 cups all-purpose flour
- 1 teaspoon baking soda
- 2 large eggs eggs, beaten

Directions

- **Step 1**
  In a saucepan, combine the water, sugar, mixed spice, cinnamon, mixed fruit, golden raisins and margarine. Bring to a boil and let simmer for one minute. Remove from the heat and stir in the flour, baking soda and eggs. Pour into a microwave-safe bowl.
- **Step 2**
  Place the bowl into the microwave, uncovered. Cook for 10 minutes on full power. Let stand for 5 minutes. Serve warm with your favorite custard.

Nutrition Facts

Per Serving:

554 calories; protein 6.7g 13% DV; carbohydrates 82.5g 27% DV; fat 24.3g 37% DV; cholesterol 46.5mg 16% DV; sodium 447mg 18% DV.

Stuffed Acorn Squash Supreme

Prep: 10 mins **Cook:** 20 mins **Total:** 30 mins **Servings:** 4 **Yield:** 4 servings

Ingredients

- 1 (6 ounce) package broccoli and cheese flavored rice mix
- 1 pound turkey breakfast sausage
- 1 medium acorn squash, halved and seeded
- ½ cup chopped apple
- 2 teaspoons crushed coriander seed
- ½ cup shredded Monterey Jack cheese

Directions

- **Step 1**
  Prepare rice mix according to package directions; cover, and set aside.
- **Step 2**
  Place squash halves cut side down onto a plate. Cook the squash in a microwave oven for 5 minutes on High, until tender but firm.
- **Step 3**
  In a medium skillet over medium heat, cook sausage until evenly browned; drain, and set aside.
- **Step 4**
  In a large bowl, mix together the prepared rice, sausage, apple, and coriander. Stuff each squash half with the mixture.
- **Step 5**
  Cover stuffed squash halves with plastic wrap, and heat in the microwave until squash is cooked through and soft, about 5 minutes. Remove plastic, and top stuffed squash with cheese. Continue to cook until cheese is melted, about 1 minute.

Nutrition Facts

Per Serving:

532.4 calories; protein 33.7g 67% DV; carbohydrates 43.1g 14% DV; fat 27.1g 42% DV; cholesterol 107.8mg 36% DV; sodium 1408.4mg 56% DV.

Lemon Mug Cake

Prep: 2 mins **Cook:** 5 mins **Additional:** 5 mins **Total:** 12 mins **Servings:** 2 **Yield:** 2 servings

Ingredients

- ½ cup all-purpose flour
- 1 teaspoon baking powder
- ½ teaspoon baking soda
- 1 pinch salt
- ⅓ cup milk
- ⅓ cup light brown sugar
- ½ teaspoon olive oil
- 1 small egg
- ¼ cup lemon juice
- 1 tablespoon lemon zest
- ½ teaspoon butter for greasing

Directions

- **Step 1**
  Combine flour, baking powder, baking soda, and salt in a small bowl. Whisk together milk, brown sugar, olive oil, egg, lemon juice, and lemon zest in a separate bowl. Add milk mixture to flour mixture and stir until batter is well combined, leaving a few lumps.
- **Step 2**
  Grease a large microwave-safe mug with butter. Pour batter into the mug. Microwave for 3 minutes. Remove and leave to set for 5 minutes.

Cook's Note:

Sprinkle mug cake with a mixture of lemon zest and powdered sugar for extra flavor.

Nutrition Facts

Per Serving:

329.6 calories; protein 7.1g 14% DV; carbohydrates 65.6g 21% DV; fat 5.2g 8% DV; cholesterol 74.8mg 25% DV; sodium 697.1mg 28% DV.

Chicken Enchiladas III

Prep: 20 mins **Cook:** 20 mins **Total:** 40 mins **Servings:** 8 **Yield:** 8 servings

Ingredients

- 1 (1 pound) loaf processed cheese food, cubed

- 1 (16 ounce) container sour cream
- 2 (10.75 ounce) cans condensed cream of chicken soup
- 8 fluid ounces evaporated milk
- 1 teaspoon ground cumin
- 1 (10 ounce) can chicken chunks, drained
- 2 cups shredded Cheddar cheese
- 1 (4 ounce) can chopped green chile peppers
- 10 (10 inch) flour tortillas

Directions

- **Step 1**
  Preheat oven to 350 degrees F (175 degrees C).
- **Step 2**
  In a medium size microwave safe bowl, combine the processed cheese food, sour cream, 1 can of soup, and evaporated milk. Stir together, and heat in microwave oven until smooth, stirring at intervals. Add cumin to taste, and set aside.
- **Step 3**
  In a medium size bowl, combine the chicken, remaining can of soup, shredded cheese, and green chile peppers. Drop spoonfuls of chicken mixture in center of tortillas, and roll up. Place in a lightly greased 9x13 inch baking dish. Pour reserved sour cream mixture over all.
- **Step 4**
  Bake in the preheated oven for 20 minutes.

Nutrition Facts

Per Serving:

885.2 calories; protein 38.7g 77% DV; carbohydrates 66.7g 22% DV; fat 45g 69% DV; cholesterol 136.4mg 46% DV; sodium 2217.7mg 89% DV.

Spooky Halloween Eyeballs

Prep: 20 mins **Additional:** 3 hrs **Total:** 3 hrs 20 mins **Servings:** 30 **Yield:** 30 servings

Ingredients

- 1 ½ cups creamy peanut butter
- ½ cup butter, softened
- 2 ½ cups confectioners' sugar, sifted
- 1 tablespoon vanilla extract
- 12 ounces white chocolate, chopped
- 2 tablespoons shortening
- 2 drops blue food coloring
- ½ cup miniature semisweet chocolate chips
- 2 drops red food coloring

Directions

- **Step 1**
  Beat the peanut butter and butter with an electric mixer in a large bowl until smooth. Beat in the sugar and vanilla. Cover and refrigerate for 30 minutes. Roll chilled dough into small, eyeball-sized balls and place on 2 baking sheets lined with wax paper. Refrigerate for another 30 minutes.
- **Step 2**
  Melt the white chocolate and shortening in a microwave-safe glass or ceramic bowl in 30-second intervals, stirring after each melting, for 1 to 3 minutes (depending on your microwave). Do not overheat or chocolate will scorch. Dip each eyeball into the white chocolate and transfer to the waxed paper until the chocolate has set. You can chill them in the refrigerator.
- **Step 3**
  Stir a few drops of blue food coloring into the remaining melted white chocolate. Make a round "iris" on the top of the cooled eyeball and press a mini chocolate chip in the center for a "pupil." For an extra spooky bloodshot eyeballs take a toothpick dipped in red food coloring and make squiggly lines on the eye.

Nutrition Facts

Per Serving:

226.6 calories; protein 4g 8% DV; carbohydrates 21.4g 7% DV; fat 14.9g 23% DV; cholesterol 10.5mg 4% DV; sodium 91.5mg 4% DV.

Escargot Mushrooms

Prep: 5 mins **Cook:** 5 mins **Total:** 10 mins **Servings:** 6 **Yield:** 6 servings

Ingredients

- 4 tablespoons butter
- 2 cloves garlic, minced
- 6 eaches helix snails, without shells
- 6 large fresh mushrooms

Directions

- **Step 1**
  Over medium heat in a medium saucepan, heat butter and garlic. Place the snails in the saucepan and slowly cook until tender, about 5 minutes.
- **Step 2**
  Remove and discard mushroom stems. Fill the mushroom caps with 1/2 teaspoon melted butter with garlic from the saucepan. Microwave 2 to 3 minutes. Insert the snails in the mushroom caps. Microwave another 3 minutes.

Nutrition Facts

Per Serving:

88.1 calories; protein 3.2g 7% DV; carbohydrates 1.9g 1% DV; fat 7.8g 12% DV; cholesterol 26.9mg 9% DV; sodium 73.4mg 3% DV.

Easy Cashew Sea Salt Toffee

Prep: 5 mins **Cook:** 8 mins **Additional:** 47 mins **Total:** 1 hr **Servings:** 8 **Yield:** 1 9-inch disk toffee

Ingredients

- ½ cup butter or margarine
- 1 ¼ teaspoons Diamond Crystal Sea Salt, divided
- 1 cup sugar
- ¼ cup water
- ¾ cup coarsely chopped cashews, divided
- ¾ cup milk chocolate chips or chopped milk chocolate

Directions

- **Step 1**
  Butter the top edges of a 2-quart microwave-safe casserole. Add butter, 1 teaspoon of the Diamond Crystal Sea Salt, sugar, and water to the casserole. DO NOT STIR. Microwave on high for 6 to 8 minutes. Check contents for color change. Continue microwaving on high a minute at a time until the mixture just begins to turn a tan color. You need to watch it carefully, and remember: DON'T STIR.
- **Step 2**
  Sprinkle 1/2 cup of the chopped cashews into a 9-into circle on a Silpat mat, parchment paper, or on a buttered baking sheet
- **Step 3**
  Carefully pour the liquid mixture evenly over the top of the cashews. Immediately sprinkle on the chocolate chips. Allow to sit for 1 minute to melt the chocolate.
- **Step 4**
  Use spatula to smooth out chocolate over the entire sheet of candy.
- **Step 5**
  Sprinkle the remaining cashews and 1/4 teaspoon Diamond Crystal Sea Salt over the top. Refrigerate to cool completely. When cool, break into bite-sized pieces. Store tightly covered in refrigerator.

Tips

If the butter releases from the toffee, it probably cooked a bit too long. When it happens I just tilt the pan so that the butter runs away from the toffee before it cools. Works well with other nuts and chocolate combinations also.

Nutrition Facts

Per Serving:

356.2 calories; protein 3.1g 6% DV; carbohydrates 38.7g 13% DV; fat 22.7g 35% DV; cholesterol 35.8mg 12% DV; sodium 575.7mg 23% DV.

The Best White Chocolate Almond Bark

Prep: 5 mins **Cook:** 12 mins **Additional:** 1 hr **Total:** 1 hr 17 mins **Servings:** 24 **Yield:** 24 pieces

Ingredients

- 1 ¼ cups whole almonds
- 3 cups white chocolate melting wafers
- 3 tablespoons butter
- 1 teaspoon almond extract

Directions

- **Step 1**
  Preheat oven to 375 degrees F (190 degrees C). Line 2 baking sheets with parchment paper.
- **Step 2**
  Roast almonds on 1 baking sheet in the preheated oven, stirring occasionally, until toasted, about 10 minutes.
- **Step 3**
  Microwave white chocolate melting wafers and butter in a microwave-safe bowl on medium-high for 1 minute 30 seconds; stir. Microwave until completely melted, 20 to 30 seconds more. Add almond extract and stir until smooth. Stir in toasted almonds.
- **Step 4**
  Spread chocolate mixture evenly onto the second baking sheet. Chill in the refrigerator until hardened, about 1 hour. Break into small pieces by hand.

Nutrition Facts

Per Serving:

170.5 calories; protein 2.8g 6% DV; carbohydrates 14g 5% DV; fat 12g 19% DV; cholesterol 8.3mg 3% DV; sodium 29.4mg 1% DV.

Asparagus Lasagna

Prep: 20 mins **Cook:** 10 mins **Total:** 30 mins **Servings:** 4 **Yield:** 4 servings

Ingredients

- 5 noodles wide lasagna noodles
- 2 tablespoons margarine
- 2 cloves garlic, chopped
- 2 tablespoons all-purpose flour
- 1 ½ cups milk
- ½ teaspoon dried thyme
- 1 (15 ounce) can asparagus, drained

- 1 cup julienned fully cooked ham
- 1 cup shredded mozzarella cheese

Directions

- **Step 1**
  Bring a large pot of lightly salted water to a boil. Cook lasagna noodles in boiling water for 8 to 10 minutes, or until al dente. Drain, and cut noodles in half crosswise.
- **Step 2**
  Melt margarine in a skillet over medium heat. Saute garlic just until fragrant. Stir in the flour until no lumps remain. Gradually mix in milk, and season with thyme. Simmer sauce gently until thick. Remove from heat.
- **Step 3**
  Grease a 9x9 inch glass baking dish. Layer noodles, sauce, asparagus, ham, and mozzarella cheese in three layers, each starting with noodles, and ending with shredded cheese on the top.
- **Step 4**
  Cover the dish, and cook in the microwave on HIGH for 9 to 10 minutes, or until cheese is melted and bubbly. Time may vary depending on the oven used. Let stand for 5 to 10 minutes before serving.

Nutrition Facts

Per Serving:

388 calories; protein 22.6g 45% DV; carbohydrates 33.2g 11% DV; fat 18.8g 29% DV; cholesterol 44.3mg 15% DV; sodium 1008mg 40% DV.

Miracle Chocolate-Coffee Icing Green Tea Mousse Cheesecake

Prep: 20 mins **Cook:** 1 min **Additional:** 7 hrs **Total:** 7 hrs 21 mins **Servings:** 12 **Yield:** 1 9-inch cheesecake

Ingredients

- 1 (4.8 ounce) package graham crackers, crushed
- 2 tablespoons white sugar
- 3 tablespoons unsalted butter, melted
- 2 tablespoons green tea powder (matcha)
- ½ cup warm water
- 2 tablespoons unflavored gelatin
- ½ cup cold water
- 2 cups whipping cream
- 2 (8 ounce) packages cream cheese, at room temperature

- ½ cup white sugar
- 1 teaspoon vanilla extract
- ¼ cup honey
- 2 large eggs eggs

Directions

- **Step 1**
  Combine the graham cracker crumbs with 2 tablespoons of sugar in a mixing bowl. Drizzle in the melted butter and mix until evenly moistened. Press into the bottom of a 9-inch springform pan lined with waxed paper; set aside.
- **Step 2**
  Stir the tea powder into the warm water; set aside. Sprinkle the gelatin over the cold water; set aside.
- **Step 3**
  Whip the cream to stiff peaks; set aside. Beat the cream cheese, 1/2 cup sugar, vanilla, and honey in a clean mixing bowl. Beat in the eggs one at a time until evenly blended. Cook the gelatin mixture in the microwave until melted, about 45 seconds. Beat the gelatin and tea into the cream cheese mixture, then fold in the whipped cream until smooth. Pour into the springform pan. Refrigerate 7 hours to overnight before unmolding and serving.

Nutrition Facts

Per Serving:

416.8 calories; protein 5.7g 11% DV; carbohydrates 27.4g 9% DV; fat 32.6g 50% DV; cholesterol 134mg 45% DV; sodium 207.5mg 8% DV.

Easy Spicy Udon Cold Salad

Prep: 25 mins **Cook:** 2 mins **Additional:** 4 hrs **Total:** 4 hrs 27 mins **Servings:** 4 **Yield:** 4 servings

Ingredients

- 1 (7 ounce) package fresh udon noodles (such as Ka-Me)
- ½ (14.5 ounce) can bean sprouts, drained
- ½ onion, thinly sliced
- 1 carrot, grated
- ½ (4.5 ounce) can mushroom pieces, drained
- 1 bunch fresh cilantro, chopped, or to taste
- 2 teaspoons sesame seeds
- 3 tablespoons rice vinegar
- 3 tablespoons soy sauce
- 1 tablespoon olive oil
- 1 tablespoon sesame oil
- 1 tablespoon white sugar, or to taste
- 1 tablespoon diced ginger

- 1 teaspoon minced garlic
- 1 splash lime juice
- 1 splash white wine
- 1 dash sriracha sauce
- 1 pinch red pepper flakes, or to taste

Directions

- **Step 1**
  Remove udon noodles from outer bag. Pierce inner pouch several times and place on a microwave-safe plate. Cook in the microwave until tender, about 90 seconds.
- **Step 2**
  Transfer noodles to a large bowl. Mix in bean sprouts, onion, carrot, mushrooms, cilantro, and sesame seeds.
- **Step 3**
  Mix rice vinegar, soy sauce, olive oil, sesame oil, sugar, ginger, garlic, lime juice, white wine, sriracha sauce, and red pepper flakes together in a small bowl until sugar dissolves. Pour dressing over the noodle mixture in the bowl; toss to combine. Refrigerate until flavors combine, at least 4 hours.

Nutrition Facts

Per Serving:

273.3 calories; protein 6.2g 12% DV; carbohydrates 40.7g 13% DV; fat 8.4g 13% DV; cholesterolmg; sodium 1085.2mg 43% DV.

Keto Peanut Butter Bars

Prep: 10 mins **Cook:** 5 mins **Additional:** 1 hr **Total:** 1 hr 15 mins **Servings:** 16 **Yield:** 16 bars

Ingredients

- ½ cup plant based butter (such as Country Crock Plant Butter)
- 1 cup erythritol confectioners' sweetener (such as Swerve)
- 1 cup graham cracker crumbs
- ½ cup creamy peanut butter
- 1 cup dark chocolate chips (such as Lily's)
- 2 tablespoons creamy peanut butter

Directions

- **Step 1**
  Line an 8-inch square pan with parchment paper, extending the ends over the sides of the pan.
- **Step 2**
  Microwave plant based butter for 45 seconds or until melted. Add confectioners' sugar, graham cracker crumbs, and 1/2 cup peanut butter; mix well. Press into the bottom of the prepared pan.

- **Step 3**
  Microwave chocolate chips and 2 tablespoons peanut butter for 45 seconds. Stir and continue to microwave at 20 second intervals until melted. Pour over graham cracker-peanut butter mixture and spread with an offset spatula until smooth.
- **Step 4**
  Refrigerate until semi-hardened, about 30 minutes. Score chocolate layer with a knife so that chocolate layer will not crack when cutting into bars. Refrigerate until firm, about 30 more minutes.
- **Step 5**
  Remove dessert from pan by pulling on the extended parchment paper; cut into bars.

Cook's Note:

If you're not on the keto diet, these bars can be made with real butter and real powdered sugar.

Nutrition Facts

Per Serving:

182.2 calories; protein 3.5g 7% DV; carbohydrates 25.4g 8% DV; fat 14g 22% DV; cholesterolmg; sodium 146.6mg 6% DV.

Black Bean Soup with Bacon

Prep: 15 mins **Cook:** 30 mins **Total:** 45 mins **Servings:** 6 **Yield:** 6 servings

Ingredients

- 6 slices bacon
- 2 cloves garlic, minced
- 2 large carrots
- 1 large onion
- 2 stalks celery
- 2 cups water
- 2 cubes beef bouillon
- 2 (16 ounce) cans diced tomatoes
- 3 (15 ounce) cans black beans, rinsed and drained
- 2 tablespoons ground cumin
- 5 dashes hot pepper sauce
- 1 pinch salt to taste
- ¼ cup sour cream, for topping
- ½ cup shredded Cheddar cheese

Directions

- **Step 1**
  Fry the bacon in a microwave until crisp, or cook it in a skillet over medium-high heat, turning occasionally, until evenly browned, about 10 minutes. Drain the bacon slices on a paper towel-lined plate, crumble, and set aside. Reserve 1 tablespoon of bacon drippings, if desired.

- **Step 2**
  Roughly chop the carrots, onion, and celery and transfer to a food processor. Pulse the vegetables until finely chopped.
- **Step 3**
  In a microwave-safe bowl, combine the reserved bacon drippings (if using), the chopped vegetables, garlic, water, bouillon cubes, and 1 can of diced tomatoes with their juice. Cook on high for 5 minutes to soften vegetables.
- **Step 4**
  Pour the vegetable mixture into a saucepan and add 2 cans of rinsed and drained black beans. Season with the cumin, hot sauce, and salt. Bring the mixture to a boil and then reduce the heat to low; simmer for 15 minutes.
- **Step 5**
  Use an immersion blender to puree the hot mixture. (If you don't have a hand-held blender, puree the mixture in batches in a food processor or standard blender.)
- **Step 6**
  Stir in the remaining can of diced tomatoes and can of black beans. Taste and adjust the seasonings. Add water if the consistency is too thick for your liking. Bring the soup to a simmer and heat for 5 minutes. Ladle the soup into bowls and top with sour cream, shredded cheese, and crumbled bacon.

Cook's Note

You can substitute 2 cups of beef broth for the water and bouillon cubes, if desired.

Nutrition Facts

Per Serving:

172.4 calories; protein 8.5g 17% DV; carbohydrates 12.1g 4% DV; fat 9.6g 15% DV; cholesterol 24.2mg 8% DV; sodium 857.3mg 34% DV.

Movie Theater Floor

Prep: 5 mins **Cook:** 5 mins **Additional:** 15 mins **Total:** 25 mins **Servings:** 15 **Yield:** 15 servings

Ingredients

- 4 cups popped popcorn
- ½ (10.5 ounce) bag corn chips (such as Fritos)
- ½ (14 ounce) package candy corn
- 1 (10 ounce) can mixed nuts
- 1 cup jelly beans or other small candies, or as desired
- 1 (12 ounce) package white chocolate chips

Directions

- **Step 1**
  Mix popcorn, corn chips, candy corn, mixed nuts, and jelly beans together in a large bowl.
- **Step 2**

In a microwave-safe glass bowl, melt the white chocolate chips on Low setting until barely melted, 1 or 2 minutes. Stir until smooth. Pour the white chocolate over the popcorn mixture, and stir to coat. Allow to cool, and break apart into small pieces.

Nutrition Facts

Per Serving:

420 calories; protein 5.8g 12% DV; carbohydrates 50.7g 16% DV; fat 22.5g 35% DV; cholesterol 4.8mg 2% DV; sodium 250.7mg 10% DV.

Dan's Meat Wrap

Prep: 9 mins **Cook:** 1 min **Total:** 10 mins **Servings:** 1 **Yield:** 1 serving

Ingredients

- 1 (10 inch) flour tortilla
- 4 slices roast beef
- ½ cup shredded Cheddar-Monterey Jack cheese blend
- ½ cup shredded lettuce
- ½ cup chopped tomato
- ¼ cup chopped onion
- 4 eaches black olives
- 2 tablespoons Italian-style salad dressing

Directions

- **Step 1**
- Place tortilla on a plate. Cover tortilla with roast beef, then cheese. Microwave for 45 seconds, or until cheese is melted. Sprinkle with lettuce, tomato, onion and olives. Top with 3 or 4 splashes Italian dressing. Roll up.

Nutrition Facts

Per Serving:

698.8 calories; protein 42.7g 85% DV; carbohydrates 53.1g 17% DV; fat 35.8g 55% DV; cholesterol 104.6mg 35% DV; sodium 2616.2mg 105% DV.

Chocolate Hummus

Prep: 10 mins **Total:** 10 mins **Servings:** 16 **Yield:** 16 servings

Ingredients

- ¼ cup milk chocolate chips
- 1 (15 ounce) can garbanzo beans, drained and rinsed
- ½ cup unsweetened cocoa powder
- 2 tablespoons maple syrup, or to taste
- 1 teaspoon vanilla extract
- ½ teaspoon salt

- 2 tablespoons almond milk, or more as needed

Directions

- **Step 1**
  Place chocolate chips in a microwave-safe bowl and heat in the microwave until melted, 1 to 3 minutes.
- **Step 2**
  Combine melted chocolate chips, garbanzo beans, cocoa powder, maple syrup, vanilla extract, and salt in the bowl of a food processor. Add almond milk 1 tablespoon at a time while blending to desired smoothness.

Nutrition Facts

Per Serving:

48 calories; protein 1.6g 3% DV; carbohydrates 8.9g 3% DV; fat 1.4g 2% DV; cholesterol 0.6mg; sodium 127.1mg 5% DV.

Espresso Bark

Prep: 10 mins**Cook** 15 min **Total** 25 min **Servings:** 12 **Yield:** 12 servings

Ingredients

- 2 cups semisweet chocolate chips
- 1 teaspoon margarine
- ¾ cup whole coffee beans
- ¼ cup chopped white chocolate

Directions

- **Step 1**
  Cover a cookie sheet with waxed paper.
- **Step 2**
  Combine the chocolate chips and margarine in a microwave-safe bowl. Heat in the microwave at 30 second intervals, stirring between each, until melted and smooth. Mix in the coffee beans until evenly distributed.

Step 3

- Pour the chocolate out onto the waxed paper and spread into an even layer. Sprinkle the pieces of white chocolate evenly over the top and press in lightly to make sure they stick. Place in the freezer until set, about 5 minutes. Break into pieces and store in an airtight container.

Nutrition Facts

Per Serving:

159.6 calories; protein 1.5g 3% DV; carbohydrates 20.4g 7% DV; fat 9.9g 15% DV; cholesterol 0.8mg; sodium 13mg 1% DV.

Lavender Truffles

Prep: 25 mins **Cook:** 15 mins **Additional:** 3 hrs 20 mins **Total:** 4 hrs **Servings:** 16 **Yield:** 16 truffles

Ingredients

- 12 sprig (blank)s fresh lavender flower heads
- ⅓ cup heavy cream
- 6 ounces bittersweet chocolate, chopped
- 4 ounces semisweet chocolate, chopped
- 2 tablespoons unsalted butter

Directions

- **Step 1**
  Place the flower heads and cream into a small microwave safe glass bowl. Cook in the microwave on High until hot to the touch, 20 to 30 seconds. Once hot, stir the flowers with a spoon, and set aside to steep 5 minutes. Return to the microwave, and cook 10 to 20 seconds to reheat. Stir again, and set aside to steep 5 minutes more. Repeat the heating-stirring-steeping process two more times until the cream is strongly flavored with lavender.
- **Step 2**
  Combine the bittersweet chocolate with the semisweet chocolate in a microwave safe glass bowl. Divide the chocolate into equal portions, and set one portion aside. Cook the remaining chocolate in the microwave on High in 20 to 30 second increments until melted, stirring between each heating. Using a fine-mesh strainer, strain the cream into the melted chocolate; discard the flower heads and bits of lavender. Stir the cream and chocolate together until smooth. Chill in the refrigerator until somewhat firm, but not hard, about 1 hour.
- **Step 3**
  After the lavender chocolate mixture has chilled, place the remaining chocolate and butter into a microwave safe glass bowl. Cook in the microwave on High in 20 to 30 second increments until just melted, stirring between each heating; set aside.
- **Step 4**
  Line a baking sheet with a piece of waxed paper. Roll the lavender mixture into 1 tablespoon-sized balls, and dip into the melted chocolate mixture using a skewer or toothpick. Place onto the prepared baking sheet, and chill in the refrigerator at least 2 hours to harden.

Nutrition Facts

Per Serving:

124.5 calories; protein 1.4g 3% DV; carbohydrates 10.3g 3% DV; fat 9.1g 14% DV; cholesterol 11.1mg 4% DV; sodium 13.3mg 1% DV.

Corn with Jalapenos

Prep: 15 mins **Cook:** 6 mins **Total:** 21 mins **Servings:** 4 **Yield:** 4 servings

Ingredients

- 6 ears fresh corn, kernels cut from cob
- 2 medium (blank)s fresh jalapeno peppers, seeded and diced
- ⅓ cup diced onion
- 2 tablespoons chopped pimento peppers
- 2 tablespoons butter, cut into pieces
- 1 pinch salt and ground black pepper to taste

Directions

- **Step 1**

  Combine corn, jalapenos, onion, pimentos, and butter in microwave safe bowl. Cover, and cook in the microwave on 100% power until heated through, about 4 minutes depending on your microwave. Stir every minute. Serve hot.

Nutrition Facts

Per Serving:

176.1 calories; protein 4.7g 9% DV; carbohydrates 27.7g 9% DV; fat 7.4g 11% DV; cholesterol 15.3mg 5% DV; sodium 62.6mg 3% DV.

Milky Way Cupcake Icing

Prep: 5 mins **Cook:** 5 mins **Total:** 10 mins **Servings:** 15 **Yield:** 15 servings

Ingredients

- 4 (2.05 ounce) bars milk chocolate covered caramel and nougat candy bars (e.g. Milky Way)
- ¼ cup butter
- 1 tablespoon milk
- 2 teaspoons vanilla extract
- 1 ¼ cups confectioners' sugar

Directions

- **Step 1**

  Place candy bars, butter, milk and vanilla in a microwave safe bowl and microwave on High for 30 seconds; stir. Heat for an additional 10 seconds, remove the bowl from the mircrowave and stir again. Add confectioners' sugar and stir until smooth and creamy.

Nutrition Facts

Per Serving:

139.9 calories; protein 0.7g 1% DV; carbohydrates 21.4g 7% DV; fat 5.8g 9% DV; cholesterol 9.6mg 3% DV; sodium 48.2mg 2% DV.

Prep: 5 mins **Cook:** 1 min **Total:** 6 mins **Servings:** 12 **Yield:** 12 servings

Ingredients

- ¾ cup dark chocolate chips
- 6 ounces coffee-flavored low-fat yogurt

Directions

- **Step 1**
  Place chocolate chips in a microwave-safe glass measuring cup; heat in microwave, stirring every 10 seconds, until melted and smooth, 1 to 2 minutes.
- **Step 2**
  Stir yogurt into melted chocolate until icing is smooth.

Cook's Notes:

This was inspired by the wonderful sour cream ganache recipe by KatieMac on this site.
I might try some other flavors of yogurt sometime, but this one worked for me. For example, you could use cherry yogurt and garnish the cake with fresh Bing cherries and whipped cream.

Nutrition Facts

Per Serving:

62.7 calories; protein 0.6g 1% DV; carbohydrates 9.4g 3% DV; fat 3g 5% DV; cholesterol 1.3mg; sodium 9.1mg.

Keto Potato Salad

Prep: 10 mins **Cook:** 6 mins **Total:** 16 mins **Servings:** 6 **Yield:** 6 servings

Ingredients

- 1 large head cauliflower
- ¾ cup light mayonnaise
- ¼ cup chopped onion
- ¼ cup dill pickle relish
- 3 tablespoons mustard
- 1 pinch salt and ground black pepper to taste

Directions

- **Step 1**
  Chop cauliflower into bite-sized pieces, discarding the stems. Transfer to a microwave-safe dish. Cover and cook on high until tender, about 6 minutes.
- **Step 2**
  Mix mayonnaise, onion, pickle relish, mustard, salt, and pepper into the cauliflower. Mash slightly to get a creamier consistency. Chill before serving.

Nutrition Facts

Per Serving:

141.2 calories; protein 3.5g 7% DV; carbohydrates 11.2g 4% DV; fat 10.4g 16% DV; cholesterol 10.5mg 4% DV; sodium 444.3mg 18% DV.

Unbelievable Vegan Mashed Potatoes

Prep: 10 mins **Cook:** 16 mins **Total:** 26 mins **Servings:** 4 **Yield:** 4 servings

Ingredients

- 3 eaches russet potatoes, peeled and cut into chunks
- 1 bay leaf
- ½ cup soy milk (such as Silk)
- 2 tablespoons vegan mayonnaise (such as Vegenaise)
- 2 tablespoons vegan margarine (such as Earth Balance)
- 1 tablespoon vegan grated Parmesan-style topping (such as Go Veggie
- 1 pinch salt and ground black pepper to taste

Directions

- **Step 1**
  Place potato chunks and bay leaf into a large pot and cover with water; bring to a boil. Reduce heat to medium-low and simmer until tender, 10 to 15 minutes. Drain and transfer to a large bowl.
- **Step 2**
  Combine soy milk, vegan mayonnaise, vegan margarine, Parmesan-style topping, salt, and pepper in a microwave-safe bowl. Heat in 30-second intervals until margarine is melted, 1 to 2 minutes.
- **Step 3**
  Pour soy milk mixture over potatoes in the bowl; mash until smooth with a potato masher.

Cook's Note:

Add more vegan Parmesan-style cheese for cheesier potatoes.

Nutrition Facts

Per Serving:

232.3 calories; protein 5.2g 10% DV; carbohydrates 31.9g 10% DV; fat 9.9g 15% DV; cholesterolmg; sodium 166.5mg 7% DV.

Texas Hash in the Microwave

Prep: 10 mins **Cook:** 25 mins **Additional:** 10 mins **Total:** 45 mins **Servings:** 4 **Yield:** 4 servings

Ingredients

- 1 pound ground beef
- 1 tablespoon minced garlic
- 1 ½ teaspoons tomato, garlic, and basil seasoning blend (such as Mrs. Dash®)
- 2 (14.5 ounce) cans no-salt-added stewed tomatoes
- 1 cup instant white rice
- ½ onion, chopped
- 1 teaspoon dried minced onion, or to taste

- ¼ cup shredded mozzarella cheese, or to taste

Directions

- **Step 1**
  Crumble ground beef into a 3-quart glass, microwave-safe, casserole dish; mix in garlic and seasoning blend. Cook on high, stirring halfway through, for 5 minutes. Drain.
- **Step 2**
  Mix stewed tomatoes, rice, chopped onion, and minced onion into ground beef mixture. Cover and cook on high, stirring halfway through, until rice is cooked through, about 20 minutes. Let stand, covered, for 10 minutes. Stir and add mozzarella cheese.

Cook's Notes:

You can also add 1/2 green pepper (chopped), 1/2 cup chopped mushrooms, and 1 can of low-sodium cream of mushroom soup.

Any variety of cheese can be used in place of the mozzarella cheese.

Nutrition Facts

Per Serving:

421 calories; protein 24.4g 49% DV; carbohydrates 34.8g 11% DV; fat 19.1g 29% DV; cholesterol 74.2mg 25% DV; sodium 138.4mg 6% DV.

Candy Bar Fudge

Prep: 20 mins **Cook:** 10 mins **Additional:** 2 hrs **Total:** 2 hrs 30 mins **Servings:** 32 **Yield:** 2 3/4 pounds

Ingredients

- ½ cup butter
- ⅓ cup unsweetened cocoa powder
- ¼ cup packed brown sugar
- ¼ cup milk
- 3 ½ cups confectioners' sugar
- 1 teaspoon vanilla extract
- 30 caramels individually wrapped caramels, unwrapped
- 1 tablespoon water
- 2 cups salted peanuts
- ½ cup semisweet chocolate chips
- ½ cup milk chocolate chips

Directions

- **Step 1**
  Grease an 8x8 inch square baking pan.

- **Step 2**
  In a microwave-safe bowl, combine butter, cocoa powder, brown sugar and milk. Microwave until mixture boils. Stir in confectioners' sugar and vanilla extract. Pour into prepared pan.
- **Step 3**
  In a microwave-safe bowl, microwave caramels and water until caramels melt. Stir in peanuts. Spread mixture over chocolate layer.
- **Step 4**
  In a small microwave-safe bowl, combine semisweet and milk chocolate chips; microwave until melted. Spread over caramel layer. Chill for 2 hours, or until firm.

Nutrition Facts

Per Serving:

204.8 calories; protein 3.2g 6% DV; carbohydrates 28.4g 9% DV; fat 10g 15% DV; cholesterol 9.3mg 3% DV; sodium 124.1mg 5% DV.

Zucchini Dutch Cheese Casserole

Prep: 25 mins **Cook:** 25 mins **Total:** 50 mins **Servings:** 4 **Yield:** 4 servings

Ingredients

- 2 cups egg noodles
- 4 cups diced zucchini
- ½ cup water
- ¼ cup butter or margarine
- 1 ½ cups chopped mushrooms
- ½ cup chopped onion
- 1 clove garlic, chopped
- ¼ cup flour
- ¾ teaspoon salt
- ¾ teaspoon dried basil
- 1 ½ cups milk
- 1 ½ cups shredded Gouda cheese

Directions

- **Step 1**
  Bring a large pot of lightly salted water to a boil over high heat. Add the egg noodles, and cook until al dente, 8 to 10 minutes. Drain in a colander, rinse with cold water, and set aside.
- **Step 2**
  Meanwhile, place the zucchini and water into a 2 quart, microwave safe casserole dish with lid. Cover and cook in the microwave on high for 6 minutes. Scrape the zucchini into the colander with the pasta and set aside. Place the butter, mushrooms, onion, and garlic into the casserole dish. Cook

on high for 3 minutes, then stir in the flour, salt, and basil. Stir in the milk, then return the dish to the microwave and cook on high 5 minutes more, stirring every 2 minutes.

- **Step 3**
  Stir the zucchini and pasta into the mushroom sauce along with 1 cup of the Gouda cheese. Cook for 6 more minutes on high, then sprinkle with the remaining cheese, and cook another minute until the cheese has melted.

Nutrition Facts

Per Serving:

444.3 calories; protein 20.5g 41% DV; carbohydrates 32g 10% DV; fat 26.9g 41% DV; cholesterol 105.1mg 35% DV; sodium 943.6mg 38% DV.

Leftover Dog Pile

Prep: 10 mins **Cook:** 5 mins **Total:** 15 mins **Servings:** 1 **Yield:**1 dog pile

Ingredients

- 2 eaches hot dogs
- ¾ cup chili with beans
- 1 slice bread
- ¼ cup shredded Cheddar cheese, divided
- 1 tablespoon chopped onion
- 2 tablespoons prepared yellow mustard

Directions

- **Step 1**
  Place the hot dogs onto a microwave safe plate and cook in the microwave 1 to 2 minutes until hot. Place the chili into a microwave safe bowl and microwave 1 to 2 minutes until hot. Slice the hot dogs in half lengthwise, and place onto the bread slice cut-side down; sprinkle with half of the cheese, the chili, the remaining cheese, onion, and mustard.

Nutrition Facts

Per Serving:

892 calories; protein 38.8g 78% DV; carbohydrates 40.5g 13% DV; fat 66g 102% DV; cholesterol 150.3mg 50% DV; sodium 3092.3mg 124% DV.

Plantains in Butter Rum Sauce

Prep: 10 mins **Cook:** 10 mins **Total:** 20 mins **Servings:** 6 **Yield:** 6 servings

Ingredients

- Ingredient Checklist
- 1 tablespoon sliced almonds, or to taste

- ½ cup white sugar
- ¼ cup rum
- ¼ cup butter
- 2 medium (blank)s plantains, peeled and sliced
- 1 pinch ground cinnamon, or to taste

Directions

- **Step 1**
  Cook and stir almonds in a skillet over medium-high heat until golden and toasted, 2 to 4 minutes.
- **Step 2**
  Stir sugar, rum, and butter together in a microwave-safe bowl. Cover the bowl with a lid or plastic wrap and microwave until hot, stirring once, 2 to 3 minutes.
- **Step 3**
  Place plantain slices in rum sauce, sprinkle with cinnamon, cover the bowl, and microwave until plantains are hot and tender, 1 to 2 minutes more. Top with toasted almonds.

Nutrition Facts

Per Serving:

232.8 calories; protein 1.1g 2% DV; carbohydrates 36g 12% DV; fat 8.4g 13% DV; cholesterol 20.3mg 7% DV; sodium 57mg 2% DV.

Peanut Butter Cups

Prep: 10 mins **Cook:** 5 mins **Additional:** 30 mins **Total:** 45 mins **Servings:** 12 **Yield:** 12 cups

Ingredients

- 1 cup semisweet chocolate chips
- ¼ cup butter
- 1 tablespoon vegetable oil
- ¼ cup peanut butter

Directions

- **Step 1**
  Coat a small cup muffin tin with cooking spray. In a microwave-safe bowl, microwave chocolate with butter and oil, stirring often, until melted, 1 to 2 minutes. Pour about a tablespoon of the chocolate mixture into each muffin cup.
- **Step 2**
  Melt peanut butter in microwave, 30 to 40 seconds. Spoon about 1 teaspoon of melted peanut butter over chocolate in each muffin cup. Top with another tablespoon of chocolate.
- **Step 3**
  Chill in refrigerator 30 minutes, until set.

Nutrition Facts

Per Serving:

142.7 calories; protein 2g 4% DV; carbohydrates 9.9g 3% DV; fat 11.9g 18% DV; cholesterol 10.2mg 3% DV; sodium 53.5mg 2% DV.

White Chocolate-Raspberry Ganache

Prep: 5 mins **Cook:** 5 mins **Additional:** 5 mins **Total:** 15 mins **Servings:** 12 **Yield:** 12 servings

Ingredients

- 2 ounces heavy whipping cream
- 8 ounces white chocolate, chopped
- 1 teaspoon raspberry extract
- 1 drop pink gel food coloring

Directions

- **Step 1**

  Place chopped white chocolate into a heat-resistant bowl. Pour heavy cream into a microwave-safe bowl and heat in the microwave in 10 second intervals, making sure it doesn't boil. Pour hot cream over white chocolate and let sit for 3 minutes. Slowly stir until chocolate melts and combines with cream. Stir in raspberry extract and mix until smooth. Stir in food coloring.

Cook's Note:

Instead of raspberry extract, you can use 2 teaspoons of freeze-dried raspberries processed into a powder.

Nutrition Facts

Per Serving:

122.6 calories; protein 1.4g 3% DV; carbohydrates 10.8g 4% DV; fat 8.4g 13% DV; cholesterol 10.5mg 4% DV; sodium 21.7mg 1% DV.

Bella's Mac and Cheese

Servings: 10 **Yield:** 10 servings

Ingredients

- 1 (16 ounce) package macaroni
- 1 cup American cheese
- 1 (8 ounce) package extra sharp Cheddar cheese
- ½ cup butter

Directions

- **Step 1**

  Cook elbow macaroni according to package directions. Drain.

- **Step 2**
  Meanwhile, cut up butter, American cheese, and sharp cheese into 1 inch squares for easy melting. Separate butter and cheeses into two equal size portions.
- **Step 3**
  Begin with one of the butter and cheese portions, microwave on 50% power for 7 minutes. Remove from microwave and stir well. Add second portion of butter and cheese to melted mixture. Microwave an additional 7 minutes on 50% power. Remove and stir well.
- **Step 4**
  Pour cheese mixture over cooked macaroni and stir until noodles are coated with butter and cheese mixture. Allow to stand for 10 minutes before serving.

Nutrition Facts

Per Serving:

388.2 calories; protein 14.6g 29% DV; carbohydrates 34.5g 11% DV; fat 21.5g 33% DV; cholesterol 61.6mg 21% DV; sodium 420.8mg 17% DV.

Chicken Cabbage Wraps

Prep: 15 mins **Cook:** 7 mins **Total:** 22 mins **Servings:** 5 **Yield:** 5 servings

Ingredients

- 1 cup chopped celery
- ½ cup chopped carrots
- ⅓ cup chopped red bell pepper
- 12 eaches water chestnut slices
- ¼ cup low-fat sesame-ginger salad dressing (such as Walden Farms®)
- 1 tablespoon red curry paste
- 4 ounces cubed cooked chicken
- 5 large leaf (blank)s cabbage leaves

Directions

- **Step 1**
  Mix celery, carrots, bell peppers, and water chestnuts together in a microwave-safe bowl. Add sesame-ginger dressing and curry paste and toss to coat.
- **Step 2**
  Cover vegetables and microwave on high until fork tender, about 4 minutes. Stir chicken into vegetables and microwave on high until chicken is heated through, about 2 minutes.
- **Step 3**
  Place cabbage leaves in a microwave-save bowl and microwave until soft, about 1 minute. Spoon equal portions of vegetable mixture onto each cabbage leaf.

Nutrition Facts

Per Serving:

87.7 calories; protein 7.1g 14% DV; carbohydrates 9.2g 3% DV; fat 2.4g 4% DV; cholesterol 16.8mg 6% DV; sodium 263.4mg 11% DV.

Printed in Great Britain
by Amazon